MOUNTAIN PEOPLE, MOUNTAIN CRAFTS

MOUNTAIN PEOPLE, MOUNTAIN CRAFTS

Elinor Lander Horwitz

PHOTOGRAPHS BY JOSHUA HORWITZ AND
ANTHONY HORWITZ

J. B. LIPPINCOTT COMPANY/PHILADELPHIA AND NEW YORK

The author wishes to thank the following people for their invaluable contribution to this book: Margaret Parsons of the Office of Museum Programs, Smithsonian Institution; Scott Odell of the Division of Musical Instruments, Smithsonian Institution; and J. Roderick Moore, Associate Director of the Blue Ridge Institute at Ferrum College, Ferrum, Virginia.

U.S. Library of Congress Cataloging in Publication Data

Horwitz, Elinor Lander.
  Mountain people, mountain crafts.

  SUMMARY: Gives a brief history of the folk culture and crafts in the Appalachian region and discusses their present-day revival by introducing contemporary craftsmen and their work.
  1. Handicraft—Appalachian region—Juvenile literature. [1. Handicraft—Appalachian region] I. Horwitz, Joshua, illus. II. Horwitz, Anthony, illus. III. Title.
TT23.2.H67 1974   745.5'0974   73-19665
ISBN-0-397-31498-1   ISBN-0-397-31499-X (pbk.)

THIS BOOK IS DEDICATED TO
THE GIFTED AND GRACIOUS
MEN AND WOMEN OF
THE SOUTHERN MOUNTAINS
WHO TAUGHT SO MUCH TO
THREE VISITING FOREIGNERS

CONTENTS

MOUNTAIN PEOPLE, MOUNTAIN CRAFTS

APPALACHIAN CRAFTS AND CRAFTSPEOPLE

A journey through the southern Appalachian highlands, undertaken in search of the basket-maker in the hollow and the weaver on the mountaintop, is a journey into another land. Most of its citizens live out their lives cut off from material comforts and conveniences considered commonplace throughout the rest of the United States. It is a land of vivid contrasts—a land where magnificent mountain scenery gives way, just up the road, to the view of a strip-mining bulldozer which curves around the hillside, exposing rich seams of coal and sending tons of rock, dirt, and timber cascading down into streams already glutted with trash and the corpses of abandoned automobiles. On Saturdays the sidewalks of every small town in the southern mountains are crowded with farmers in bibtop overalls, who gather to exchange news on corners, by storefronts, or on benches, as they transform sticks into toothpicks with their whittling knives. And on Sundays, the powerful exhortations of evangelical preachers thunder from hundreds of small wooden mountainside churches.

Where are the southern highlands? Technically, they extend through the western part of Maryland, the entire state of West Virginia, the Blue Ridge and Allegheny Ridge of western Virginia, the coal fields of eastern Kentucky and Tennessee, western North Carolina, and small northern bits of South Carolina, Georgia, and Alabama. They are the highlands because here forty-six peaks exceed an elevation of six thousand feet above sea level. The northern part of the Appalachian chain boasts only one such height—Mount Washington in New Hampshire.

The highlander has no problem pinpointing the area. He simply calls it home, and he knows its boundaries.

"I'm a mountain man," says the woodcarver.

"I was born in these hills and so was all my kin," says the doll-maker, establishing her credentials.

"I'm not from these parts," says the quilter. "I was born up the next holler, up in Stinking Creek. That's the home place."

"I never been out of Letcher County," says the man playing the dulcimer in the last cabin up the hollow. "Hit's the place we always lived."

If you were not born in these hills you're forever a foreigner. A New Englander visiting the area in the 1920s asked a mountaineer how he would describe a European, since he had already usurped the term "foreigner" for his fellow Americans. "Oh, them's the outlandish," the man responded promptly.

The first pioneers, most of them English and Scots-Irish, arrived in the southern mountains in the early years of the eighteenth century. They found a region of startling natural beauty, rich in virgin timber, crossed with fresh rivers and sparkling mountain streams. The woods were filled with game and the land was wondrously fertile. The availability of federal land grants attracted new waves of settlement after the Revolutionary War. Using plentiful natural materials, the ingenious pioneers learned to make everything they needed: houses, furniture, clothing, bedding, utensils for the home and for the farm. They had come to farm, and they cleared the land and planted crops and lived by their own laws—removed from the surveillance of officialdom by the natural barrier of the hills.

Over the generations, the lives of the people of the southern Appalachians have been molded by this physical isolation more than by any other force. Their family feuds, back-yard stills, low standard of living, and lack of education and sophistication made backwoodsmen a familiar butt of humor and easy prey to exploiters. "Dogpatch" became a source of amusement to millions of comic strip readers across the country. But in the southern mountains the facts of life were tragic rather than comic, as hardworking farmers with no experience in business or finance sold out the timber and mining rights to their rich land for as little as fifty cents an acre.

The result of this exploitation has been financial and ecological ruin in Appalachia. Mining has become mechanized, and the result is mass unemployment. Small mountain farms cannot be worked profitably. Timber is depleted. The descendant of the pioneers is still proud of his heritage, but

he lives in a land of old men and disheartened women. His children leave the hills in great numbers for cities where they can find employment in industrial plants. Since only 30 percent of them have completed ten grades of school, as a group they are poorly equipped to escape the cycle of poverty.

What has all this to do with the crafts? The same isolation that made the land and its people poor also accounted for the strong crafts tradition in the mountains. At first the mountaineers, like all rural people, made their own quilts and axes and barrels and linen thread and clay crocks because there was no other way of obtaining them. Utility was the guiding principle, and if a high level of workmanship and taste resulted in the creation of an object of beauty as well, that was all to the good. Inevitably there were artistic men and women who took intense delight in the creation of handsomely made wooden spoons, chairs, and churns, or beautifully dyed woven coverlets, but making needed objects was part of the work routine of daily life. The raw materials were all around, free for the cutting or picking. Long after the industrial revolution brought cheap factory-made plates, trousers, blankets, and cooking pots to the rest of the country, the physical remoteness, poverty, and unworldliness of the people of the southern mountains made these domestic skills a continuing necessity.

By the late nineteenth century the china plates and tin buckets and factory-made banjos and bedcovers *did* reach the mountains, and the crafts began to die out. Interested outsiders initiated the first crafts revival as a means of providing a source of income for Appalachian men and women. Revelations about poverty in the Appalachians shocked many Americans when the federal government stepped in to combat the problem in the 1960s, but it had been over seventy-five years since the teachers, missionaries, and settlement workers of another age had begun trying to help the mountaineers to help themselves. Many of them saw in the lingering crafts tradition a potential source of economic improvement, and with their encouragement the people of the southern mountains began dusting off family looms and spinning wheels and making objects for sale.

An arts and crafts revival in England, inspired by William Morris and his followers, glorified handmade over machine-made products and influenced the taste of sophisticated buyers in this country. The revival gained momentum, and as the years went on crafts guilds and centers were established and markets for handmade goods were further expanded. Crafts shops opened near national parks, TVA dams, and other tourist attractions. Nimble-fingered women were urged to make dolls for shops in New York City's Greenwich Village; men who were skilled whittlers were encouraged to carve little animals and put them up for sale. The skills that had formerly been developed to turn available natural materials into objects needed for survival were now being employed to make saleable items of all sorts.

Nothing had really been forgotten, of course. Old women could still read their mothers' coverlet "drafts," or patterns, and many of their husbands still used white oak baskets when they went out to gather the potatoes. Quilting and rug-making were still providing satisfaction to women living lonely lives in remote areas. There were musical instrument makers all through the mountains. The secrets of vegetable dyeing had been retained.

Today there are many types of craftspeople in the highlands: elderly men and women who work at the old traditional pioneer crafts, and young university-trained carvers, weavers, silk screen artists, and textile designers. The particular focus of this book, with some exceptions, is the traditional handicrafter, who makes the same pioneer products his parents and grandparents did—and by the same methods. Some of these skillful men and women are very productive; some turn out only a few pieces each year. Some have supported themselves and their families by the sale of their products; others sell their work to supplement income from other employment; still others have taken to the crafts after retirement, for the pleasure of the work itself more than for any other reason. A few of the men and women in these pages have been interviewed before, but others live in complete obscurity.

They live in a land where the same Anglo-Saxon names repeat and repeat.

Some of these are familiar, like Mills and Marshall. Others—like Sizemore and Miracle—sound strange to the outsider. It is a land of few restaurants and no smart shops . . . a land of missionary schools which date from the 1920s . . . a land where children of illiterate parents leave ramshackle cabins, with washing machines on front porches and privies out back, to ride on newly paved roads to federally funded preschool programs . . . a land of rickety swinging bridges which cross the creek and small sooty coal stoves in the center of the living room.

The lush rhododendron blooms on the mountaintops, and large rabbits dart across the fields. The craftspeople of Appalachia greet the unannounced visting "foreigners" with surprising warmth and geniality. Products made of wood, of clay, of corn, of bark, of nuts and roots are displayed and old techniques and difficult skills explained with enthusiasm . . . as a child peers wistfully through the window . . . the chickens scratch by the door . . . the neighbors from up the hollow come to stare . . . and the old grandfather, quite drunk, embarrasses his dignified middle-aged daughter by taking out his fiddle and squeakily playing as he creakily sings, "Go tell Aunt Rhody, go tell Aunt Rhody, the old gray goose is dead."

MOUNTAIN MUSIC
AND TOYS

I ∿ DULCIMERS, BANJOS, AND FIDDLES

"There's no notes to a banjo, you just play it," is the instruction country musicians used to give to their children. The old banjos had no frets, and the old banjo players had no familiarity with musical notation, scales, or chords; music was not written down. People learned songs and styles of playing from each other. Today many of the best country musicians describe their versatility and skill as "just pickin'." Some are self-taught; most learned from "my daddy" or "by watchin' and alistenin' to the old people hereabouts."

Singing, dancing, and fiddling have been the predominant means of entertainment in the Appalachians since the earliest settlers arrived. The old tunes the settlers had brought with them remained totally uninfluenced by the classical or popular fashions of the outside world. The instrument-makers continued fashioning dulcimers when children in other parts of the country were learning to play clarinets, pianos, and trumpets. The old English "step-dancing" remained popular as dance fashions came and went in the cities. Mountain music was uninfluenced by the singing and playing of the Southern Negro, since there were so few blacks in the highlands.

When researchers interested in folklore and folk music went into remote areas of the southern highlands at the turn of the twentieth century, they found the mountain people singing ancient English and Scottish ballads no longer known in the British Isles, which had been handed down to generation after generation of children. In the 1920s and 1930s enthusiastic folk music researchers recorded hundreds of old hymns, ballads, dancing songs, and working songs for the Archive of Folk Song at the Library of Congress. Collectors, riding mules over hill and hollow, brought back cylinder recordings of ancient story-telling ballads, current mining songs, musical tales of love, adventure, banditry, railroad expansion, and strange rural happenings.

The old ballads were traditionally sung without instrumental accompaniment, to give the vocalist total freedom of expression. There were no organs in the mountain churches, and since stringed instruments were so totally associated with merrymaking, hymns also were performed by the unaccompanied voice. The first instruments played in Appalachia were the fiddle and the plucked dulcimer. The fiddle, brought over from England, has consistently through the decades and the centuries held first place in the esteem of mountain people, while other instruments have gone in and out of favor. Fiddles and dulcimers, and later banjos, were played for square dances and other social gatherings. It was not until the twentieth century that the guitar and then the mandolin and string bass became part of many country music bands.

The first banjos, played by the Southern slaves, were primitive gourd and gourdlike instruments. Similar plucked instruments with gut strings are found today in several African countries. During the nineteenth century the banjo gained popularity. In the 1830s the minstrel tradition began, and the banjo became the instrument of white musicians who played and sang the music of the South in blackface.

Commercial production of banjos began about the time of the Civil War, and the five-string banjo—with its short high-pitched thumb string— became more and more the commonly accepted standard around the country. Manufacturers worked at finding effective means of stretching the skin and keeping it taut; the old wooden inner rims were replaced with steel, and brackets were added. Folk banjos continued to be fashioned as they always had been, but as the years passed many a mountain man joyously gave up "Daddy's banjer" for a shiny new Sears Roebuck model. Some removed the frets on their manufactured instruments so they could slide their fingers freely up and down the strings in the fashion of the old mountain musicians.

By the twentieth century large banjo bands were a great hit throughout the country. The instrument's national popularity, however, died out in the 1930s, although it continued to be played in the Appalachians. The great revival came with the emergence of bluegrass music in the period immediately after the Second World War. The beginning of bluegrass is generally credited to Bill Monroe, a Kentuckian, who explains that he combined elements of jazz, mountain fiddling, and church music. Earl Scruggs, another bluegrass authority, writes that Appalachian banjo players always had a reputation for rowdiness, and that, despite the unceasing popularity of the instrument in the southern mountains, the musicians themselves were considered a thoroughly bad lot.

Fiddlers' conventions and other country music competitions are still major social and cultural events in the Appalachians, and great pride is taken in awards received. Both bluegrass and "old-time" playing are prevalent. Old-time groups are generally made up of guitar, fiddle, and banjo, and bluegrass groups may have more than one guitar plus a mandolin and a double bass. Dulcimer players are sometimes featured soloists between the group performances. Since the dulcimer player must perform in a seated position he can't bring the dulcimer up to the microphone when the melody is alternated among the various instruments, so the instrument is rarely heard with groups. One noted dulcimer player of Galax, Virginia, overcame this problem by attaching a microphone to his instrument.

Unlike the banjo, the dulcimer has always been a homemade mountain instrument. Recent widespread interest in folk music has brought Appalachian dulcimer-makers orders from every state in the Union.

"I make them like this because this shape—I believe you call it hourglass —is the one as has always been made here," says Edd Presnell of Banner Elk, North Carolina. "No two sound alike. I make them and then I listen and I don't know why. I can tell you, it doesn't have to do with what kind of wood you make it out of."

Leonard Glen, instrument-maker of nearby Sugar Grove, agrees. He has kept for himself a sweet-sounding three-stringed dulcimer of curly maple which he made about seven years ago. "It sounds better than the others. More kinda meller."

"It's a quiet instrument. They was made to be played in a one-room log cabin like the old banjers," says Franklin George, country musician of Mercer County, West Virginia. "Yet some folks calls it a 'hog fiddle.' Some's shaped like a figure eight, some triangular, some fish-shaped, some like a diamond—all different kinds. Way back, they was brought home to England by the crusaders who saw the Arabs playin' them. They was called 'rebec' in those days and some played them with a bow as well as pluckin'."

Others name the rebec as the ancestor of the violin or even of the banjo. Still others insist that the dulcimer, or "dulcimore" or "mountain zither," is an instrument of strictly American origin. Franklin George says no, and so

23

do a number of scholars who point out similarities to the Danish hulme, the German scheitholz, the Swedish hummel, and the Norwegian langleik. It is theorized that one of these instruments—or simply the memory of such a stringed instrument—arrived with the northern European immigrants who came to pioneer in the mountain areas of North Carolina, Kentucky, Virginia, and Pennsylvania.

Regardless of its origins, and despite its limitations compared to other instruments, the mountain dulcimer has been beloved in the southern Appalachians as far back as anyone can remember. It is a relatively easy instrument to play, although one authority reports that careless positioning can cause it to shoot off across the room during the speedier passages of a tune. The player plucks the strings with the right hand, using some sort of pick—traditionally a turkey quill. With the left hand the strings are pressed down or "noted," using either the finger or a small flattened "noter" made of wood. Only one or two strings are noted and the rest form a drone, as in a bagpipe—tuned to give a background to the changing notes of the melody as it's picked out. The frets are tuned to a diatonic scale so that noting the

dulcimer is like sounding out a tune on the white keys of the piano. There are any number of ways of tuning a dulcimer, and most players choose "the way my daddy did it." On a four-stringed dulcimer with two strings noted, the two will be tuned to the same note of the scale.

The instrument consists of a hollow sound chamber with soundholes in the top and a fretboard. The strings are anchored and adjusted with hand-carved wooden pegs. Dulcimer-makers are individualists, and one man's instrument may differ from another's in shape, design, shape of soundholes, and number of strings. Three-stringed instruments are the most traditional, but mountain men and women recall seeing four-, five-, and even six-stringed models long ago. (A six-stringed dulcimer is actually a three-stringed instrument with each string doubled.) Soundholes may be round holes, carved diamonds, hearts, or S shapes. The scroll that ends the neck may be simply or elaborately carved. All sorts of woods have been used, often in combination, with one wood forming the top and bottom and another the neck and sides. Walnut is popular, as are cherry, curly maple, and birdseye maple. Edd Presnell has also used rosewood, which is not grown locally, and every type of native tree including cucumber, poplar, chestnut, sassafras, and ash.

Presnell lives far from the nearest neighbor, on the very top of a tall mountain in the northwest corner of North Carolina. He has a long gray Rip Van Winkle beard, and a curvy-stemmed pipe rests in his mouth, its smoke wending up toward the brim of his cap as he works.

To make a dulcimer he first cuts the slender side pieces and puts them into a press to mold them permanently to the graceful hourglass shape. The back of the instrument is glued to the sides while they are still in the press. He then releases the press, leaving the sides and back firmly joined. The

next step is to carve and hollow the neck of the instrument and to attach it to the top, which is made in two pieces. The neck and top are firmly glued to the instrument's sides and the edges of the top are cut and shaved to exact size. The pegs are carved and the soundholes are cut in a delicate heart shape.

The instrument is sanded and then finished with one coat of tung oil. No stain is used. As many as a dozen thin coats of wax are applied after the tung oil and rubbed into the satiny surface of the instrument. Although only one or two strings are noted when playing, Presnell runs his frets the full width of the neck.

Roscoe Russell's dulcimers are larger and heavier than Presnell's and less orthodox in design. To give their tone greater carrying power, he uses both an inner bottom and an outer bottom or resonator. He also attributes increased volume to two braces he puts inside. He uses on his instruments

four steel second banjo strings which he generally tunes identically to a piano D or the top string of a banjo or an octave above the fourth string of a guitar. This method of tuning makes it easier to play the dulcimer with other instruments, since it permits the musician to perform in the key of D or G without retuning.

Roscoe Russell has played music all his life and has had his own prize-winning bluegrass band for many years. When his son Roy became an exceptional guitar player he switched to the baritone ukelele. The Russell Family album—Roscoe on uke; Roy, then fifteen, on guitar; and Bonnie, then thirteen, on dulcimer—is a fascinating display of traditional musical skill and virtuosity.

Bonnie, now fifteen, joins with her father in the tune "Ebenezer" at the family's small cabin near Galax, Virginia. Her grandmother, Lina Melton, was brought up to Washington, D. C., in 1937 to play the dulcimer for the extensive folk song archives in the Library of Congress. Her grandfather was a noted musician and instrument-maker, and her brother's playing is famous in the region. Bonnie is reputed to be the best dulcimer player in an area which is a renowned center of country music competitions, instrument-makers, and musicians.

Roscoe Russell points to the picture on the front of the Russell Family album. "You know why we're all smiling like that on the cover?" he asks.

"Bonnie and Roy and me were out there posing for the photographer and he kept pushing us further and further back because the sun was changing. It was a hot summer day and he got us way over closer and closer to the hog pen. Well, you know how it *is* near a hog pen in August. I says to Bonnie and Roy, 'Boy, I sure hope the *smell* doesn't come out in the picture!' —and we all laughed and the photographer took his shot."

Although the fiddle is the best-loved of all traditional mountain instruments, there are few fiddle-makers left in Appalachia. One of these is the Russells' neighbor Whitfield Sizemore, an energetic man who works in one of the Galax textile mills from 11 P.M. to 7 A.M., farms, and repairs and makes fiddles and mandolins. Like Russell, he repeatedly wins ribbons in the Galax Fiddlers' Convention. His band—composed of fiddle, guitar, banjo, and mandolin—has won the Virginia State championship twice in recent years.

The fiddle he's playing here on the hill behind his house is one he made himself. Like all country fiddles, it is identical in size, shape, and range to a concert violin, but the curve of the bridge is flattened to make it easier to play double stops.

The reddish color of the finish comes from a stain he mixes from a powder. The can in his workshop is labeled "Dragon's Blood." What kind of dragon does it come from?

"From a daid one, I'd say," the fiddle-maker answers laconically.

His fiddles, he claims, are made the way "that guy a long time ago, Stradivarius, made his." The back of the fiddle is carved in four graduated layers from one piece of wood, and he says there are two thicknesses in the top. Sizemore shakes the fiddle and a dry rustling can be heard.

"That there sound is the main secret of why my fiddles keep so good. What you hear inside is dried rattlesnake rattlers." He opens a box to show a collection of rattles he's saving to put in other fiddles. "When you shake it you hear them but when you're playin' they just set in the bottom. I kill the snakes on the hill out yonder behind the house. The rattlers is inside the fiddle to keep out the dampness and the spider webs. Those is two things as bothers a fiddle—dampness and spiders. You won't find many fiddles around with a tone like this one."

Like Roscoe Russell and Whit Sizemore, Kyle Creed lives on a country road outside the industrial town of Galax, Virginia. He and his wife run a grocery called the Country Store, and he works as a construction foreman as well. He is also a highly respected banjo-maker, and banjo playing is his greatest pleasure. He has cut four records in recent years.

"I grew up in this area, traveled all over the country, and come back again to live. I learned to pick on the banjer at fifteen," he says. "I made myself one—a country-style banjer with no frets. I just carved it out with a penknife and a drawing knife. We used to always use a hide—a cat hide or a groundhog hide."

He takes out a well-dried groundhog hide. "Here's one I got now. Roscoe's boy Roy killed it for me. He did it just right—hit him in the head, not the body. If you have shot in the body you ruin the hide for usin' on a banjer. Lots of times now, though, we use plastic. It makes a skin that's good in all weather and that's important. Lots of people around here know how to pick a banjer. I bet that within about a hundred miles all around here you'll find more musicians than anyplace in the world."

His own instrument, which he plays here, is open-backed. "It's more meller and plunky than the bluegrass kind. I made me this one from a nice piece of wood the postman give me. For bluegrass they like the resonator because more sound bounces out thataway. I do old-time claw hammer pickin' and strummin'. Earl Scruggs, he perfected bluegrass banjer pickin' —three-finger pickin' where you use two fingers and your thumb. That was very popular around here but now lots of young fellas are doin' old-time pickin'. There's lots of styles of pickin'. I pick up on the neck but most picks on the head and *all* the bluegrass players do. It changes the sound. Where you put the bridge on the head has everythin' to do with the sound, too. For old-time banjers I put it more near the center—for bluegrass I set the bridge back further on the head."

Today Creed makes banjos to order in either old-time or bluegrass style. He has few orders for the traditional fretless instruments today. He has made a great number of banjos in which the skin is held taut by an inner rim, but most of his banjos now have brackets. Many have Formica fretboards. He has tried all the native varieties of wood for his banjo necks and rims: wild cherry, white poplar, dogwood, apple, and, most frequently, maple.

It takes him about three days to make an instrument. To make the rim he takes a 2½-inch-wide strip of wood, boils it, and bends it around a steel template while it's hot and wet. He places it in the oven at 350° and then lets it cool. Two more wooden layers are added in the same way, one ⅛ inch thick and the other ¼ inch.

Then he takes the rim off the template and trues it up on the lathe. He uses two brass rods to control the spring on the neck. A tone ring fits under the head, between the rim and the head. A brass tension hook tightens the head. A lag screw holds the neck to the rim. For an eleven-inch instrument he uses sixteen brackets; for a twelve-inch he uses eighteen.

Edd Presnell makes his banjos by an entirely different method. He does not bend the wood for the rim but rather cuts a circle in a thick plank with

a bandsaw. He uses a back piece, but it has a large hole in the center. For this fretless unbracketed old-type banjo, a calfskin will form the head and a metal band will hold it tightly stretched.

"The band is going to go in right here," he explains, "to hold the skin. Then the back goes on thisaway and that presses the band down and holds the head tight. The hole in the back lets the sound out."

DISCOGRAPHY

This brief listing of fine recordings of traditional American music is a personal selection prepared for this book by Scott Odell of the Division of Musical Instruments, Smithsonian Institution. Most of the performers are musicians from the area near the Blue Ridge around Galax, Virginia, and the nearby mountains of North Carolina. The Folkways and Library of Congress albums give a broader picture of the whole range of traditional music being played and sung in the 1920s and 1930s when they were first recorded.

CLAWHAMMER BANJO: Wade Ward, Kyle Creed, George Stoneman,
  Fred Cockerham   County 701
DOWN TO THE CIDER MILL: Fred Cockerham, Thomas Jarrell,
  Oscar Jenkins   County 713
MORE CLAWHAMMER BANJO: Oscar Wright, Sidna and Fulton
  Myers, others   County 717
BACK HOME IN THE BLUE RIDGE: Fred Cockerham, Thomas
  Jarrell, Oscar Jenkins   County 723

THE RUSSELL FAMILY: Roscoe, Roy, and Bonnie Russell   County 734

County Records are available in record stores or from County Records,
307 E. 37th Street, New York, New York 10016.

ANTHOLOGY OF AMERICAN FOLK MUSIC: 3 VOLUMES   Folkways 2951, 2952, 2953
TRADITIONAL MUSIC FROM GRAYSON AND CARROLL COUNTIES   Folkways 3811

Folkways Records are available in record stores.

ANGLO-AMERICAN SHANTIES, LYRIC SONGS, DANCE TUNES AND
SPIRITUALS. Library of Congress Archive of Folk
Song.   Library of Congress L2

There are 66 records in this series of field recordings, of which
about 20 have Appalachian music. The records must be ordered direct
from the Library of Congress. A list of the records is available on
request.

II ～ DOLLS

Up the mountain, down the hollow, and around the bend, women can be found making dolls for their children and dolls for sale. Doll-making is one of the most commonly practiced crafts in the southern Appalachian Mountains today and one of the most varied. Some of the dolls are crude; others are expressions of the highest level of craftsmanship and artistry.

The early settlers fashioned wooden "poppets" for their children. Wood was the most abundant raw material in the mountains, and every mountain man knew, of necessity, how to work with it. The poppets were generally made from tight-grained buckeye, which is still popular with carvers, particularly in eastern Kentucky. The uncuddly dolls were often given soft squirrelskin wigs to make them more appealing.

Appalachia's doll-makers are continuing the tradition of using readily available materials, and their dolls are made from an astonishing range of homely ingredients. Mr. and Mrs. Nuthead's faces are simply painted on hickory nuts—the point at the bottom of the nut becomes the tip of the nose —and they wear carefully hand-sewn clothes. Some nut-headed dolls stand erect on wooden clothespin bodies anchored on round wooden discs, and they, too, are carefully costumed. Another kind of doll has a head made of a chunk of corn cob, which could just as well have been used for the bowl of a pipe. The elderly couple seated side by side have faces made of a

combination of white bread dough and glue. These dolls are from the collection of Lila Marshall of Nickelsville, Virginia.

Sometimes the simple design of a doll echoes the homely nature of the material it was made from. Huggable dolls are made from scraps, socks, buttons, and cotton batting. Among the most readily available and easily worked materials is corn husks; these two charmers have fine, frizzy corn silk hair. These dolls were photographed at the O.E.O. crafts shop in Bar-

bourville, Kentucky. More commonly seen today, however, are sophisticated, meticulously fashioned collectors' items—more appropriate for display than for playthings—such as these storybook characters, Red Riding Hood and the Wolf and Alice and the White Rabbit, made by Mrs. Emma Marshall.

Emma Marshall is the mother-in-law of Mrs. Gannell Marshall and the sister-in-law of Mrs. Lila Marshall. All are expert doll-makers. Emma Marshall's three daughters and three daughters-in-law have all worked at doll-making and other crafts. The coal mining area of southwestern Virginia in which they live must be one of the most prolific crafts centers in the country. The local crafts guilds which the doll-makers have organized afford them meeting places where craftspeople of all sorts can work together, exchange patterns, and share ideas on how to improve and market their work. The dolls are sold by mail and in shops which specialize in Appalachian crafts.

Still, the doll-makers are not easy people to find. To visit Emma and Gannell Marshall one must drive to the small sooty town of St. Paul, Virginia, and then head out of town about ten miles to the place where a road takes off to the right and winds its way to the top of Banner Mountain. The scenery is natural beauty despoiled and desecrated by both underground mining and strip mining. The narrow road goes round and round the mountain with no guard rails along the edge. It seems improbable that anyone could really live up there, and yet an entire community lies at the very top of the mountain. Take the turn by the Regular Baptist Church to find

Emma Marshall's cozy house, which sits by a woods filled with giant rhododendron.

Mrs. Marshall serves warm moist molasses cake at the kitchen table. "When my husband was alive and before the girls were married the five of us used to sit around this table and make dolls together. He was too sick with black lung disease to work in the mines any more. Then the girls married and he and I worked here together, just the two of us. Three years ago he died," she says, "and it seemed so lonely and quiet to be sitting here by myself making dolls. It still seems strange."

Mrs. Marshall was born a Kilgore, and the Kilgores once owned most of Banner Mountain. She makes apple head and corn shuck dolls and has been doing so since the early 1920s. During the depression years the sale of her dolls in a crafts shop in New York City brought in desperately needed income. Her work also provided support for her family during the long battle for black lung compensation payments.

Mrs. Marshall takes great pride in her workmanship and skill, and cheerfully demonstrates her technique. For apple heads she prefers Golden Delicious apples—not the perfect giant variety sold in supermarkets everywhere, but the small round rejects, which are just the right size. She also uses Jonathan apples and Maiden Blush and specifies that other types will do but that you must have a dry variety.

The first step in making the head is to peel the apple and then slice out the major planes of the face. A plane is cut down and in for the forehead, out for the nose. The nose is then crudely carved in a broad wedge shape, and slits are made for the eyes. The sides of the face must be sliced down into flat planes. Then ear flaps must be cut. The head is then ready for drying.

Mrs. Marshall soaks the head in salt water and then in lemon juice to avoid discoloration and to repel worms. It is then suspended over a coal

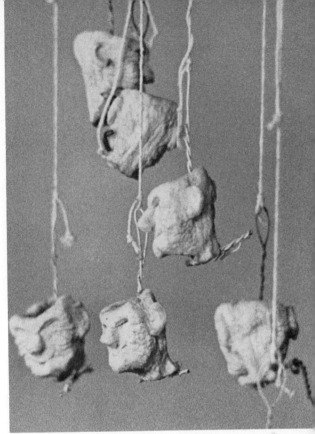

stove, hot air register, or radiator to dry. There must be air circulating for proper drying so in summer Mrs. Marshall uses an electric fan. If the head dries too slowly it will rot.

After one day the head feels spongy and damp, rather like clay, and can begin to be "worked" with the fingers. Apple head dolls are supposed to look like elderly people, and with a little careful pinching and squeezing the nose, the eyes, and the mouth can be shaped and the wrinkles will fall into place. It takes three to four days for the face to dry completely. When dry, it will be about one-half the size of the original apple.

Once the head is ready, she makes the armature for the body. She punches two holes through the apple from bottom to top using a nail, and then runs a twelve-inch piece of thin pliable wire up through one hole and down through the other so that it hooks over the top of the core. Another wire, twisted around the first at shoulder level, will support the arms. The figure is then ready to be wrapped in corn husk clothing.

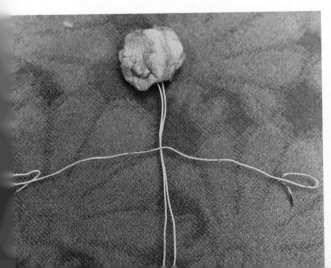

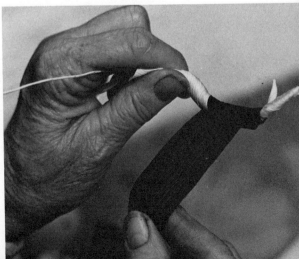

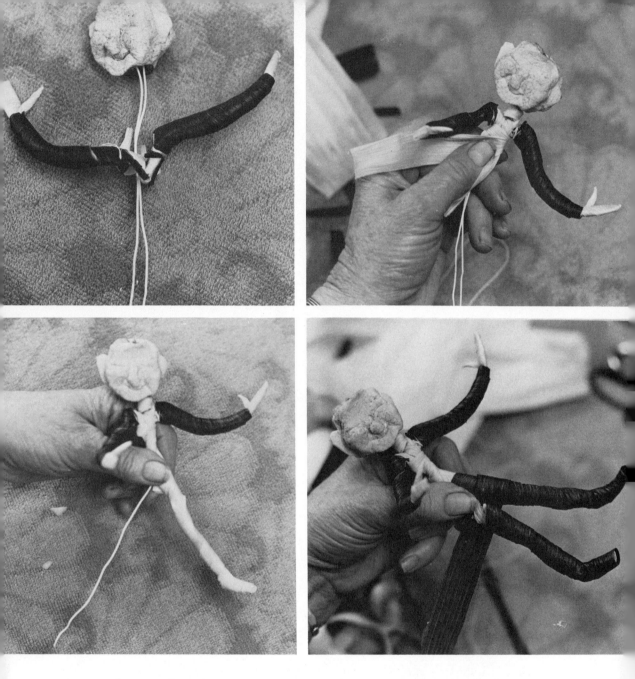

The completed figure of Grandpa has black shoes, a red shirt, green trousers, a dark blue jacket. His arms and legs are bent into position and he is seated, pipe in hand, in the corn stalk chair. His glasses are made of the same coated wire, bent into shape with the ends of the ear pieces poked into the apple just behind the hairline. His hair is cotton, glued on, and his eyes are drawn in with black ink. A bit of poster paint applied with a toothpick gives a rosy gleam to his mouth and cheeks.

Apple head dolls are also found dressed in hand-sewn clothes. Mrs. Marshall used to make them that way but found it too time-consuming.

It takes this very experienced doll-maker less than ten minutes to dress Grandpa in his colorful costume.

Mrs. Marshall's sister, Sarah Mc-Clellan, made this apple-headed grandmother, who sits in her corn stalk chair churning her butter, quite indifferent to the fact that her apron and petticoat are edged with hand-made lace.

It was twenty years ago that Emma Marshall taught her sister-in-law Lila Marshall how to make corn shuck dolls. Also a widow, Lila Marshall lives a bit south of St. Paul on a small country road outside the town of Nickelsville. She is another astonishingly nimble-fingered woman, who puts together a doll so swiftly and gracefully and with so little waste motion that watching her is almost like viewing an acrobatic performance.

Lila Marshall is a member of the Southern Highlands Handicrafts Guild, as is Emma Marshall. She is the founder of the local Clinch Valley Handicrafts Center, which started with eight members in 1959 and now has more than forty, who weave, spin, quilt, make dolls, weave chair seats, make shaved wooden flowers. Since she became a widow she has supported herself entirely with her doll-making. She attends all regional fairs as the senior member of a family booth which is also occupied by her doll-making daughter-in-law Betty; her two daughters, who make corn shuck flowers; and her son, who carves tiny figures out of peach seeds and other natural materials. Her corn shuck boys and girls, storybook characters, and figures of old-time mountaineers have been bought by people in thirty-six states and have been displayed at the Smithsonian Institution in Washington, D. C.

She shows a picture of herself and her sister, spinner and weaver Golda Porter, meeting Lady Bird Johnson when they demonstrated doll-making and spinning during a tour of Virginia that Mrs. Johnson made while First Lady. Mrs. Marshall's demonstrations at fairs have brought her into contact with all sorts of people who never come to Nickelsville—the First Lady, three governors and their wives, a woman from East Pakistan who asked to be taught how to make dolls so that she in turn might teach others and women halfway around the world could learn to do as Mrs. Marshall has done—to turn doll-making into a profitable craft, a means of self-support. "It's been a great pleasure to me," Mrs. Marshall says, "to have been able to work in my own home, making things with my own hands and supporting myself. I've always liked doing hand work, particularly working with native materials—making something out of nothing."

Husks for doll-making must be gathered from fully ripened corn which is well past the eating stage. The husks will mildew if left damp; they must be carefully picked, then flattened and permitted to dry before being stored.

Lila Marshall uses the same flexible coated "dynamite wire" her sister-in-law uses. This is easily available in mining areas, but similar wire can be found in hardware stores.

A large basket of brightly colored husks, which have been prepared in advance, is drawn over to the table. The husks are dyed with commercial vegetable dyes, following the conventional directions for fabric. The dye water must be hot and the husks are then stirred until they attain the desired hue—a bit darker, because they do fade slightly. They must then be carefully dried again before storing.

To make the doll she begins by dampening husks slightly and quickly in a basin of water. Each husk must be slightly dampened before using or it will be too brittle for wrapping. A strip of husk about one inch wide is folded over and another is wrapped around it to form the head. This knob is used as the skeleton and then a smooth husk is used to cover it. This will be the face and must be perfectly smooth because the features will later be drawn on in ink. It is tied securely at the base to form a neck. At each stage the husks must be tied into place.

Next, two strips of wire seven inches long are cut and inserted into the head from below. A five-inch piece of wire is cut as support for the shoulders and arms. This is inserted horizontally through the neck. The shoulders and arms are wrapped with narrow strips of husk round and round and up

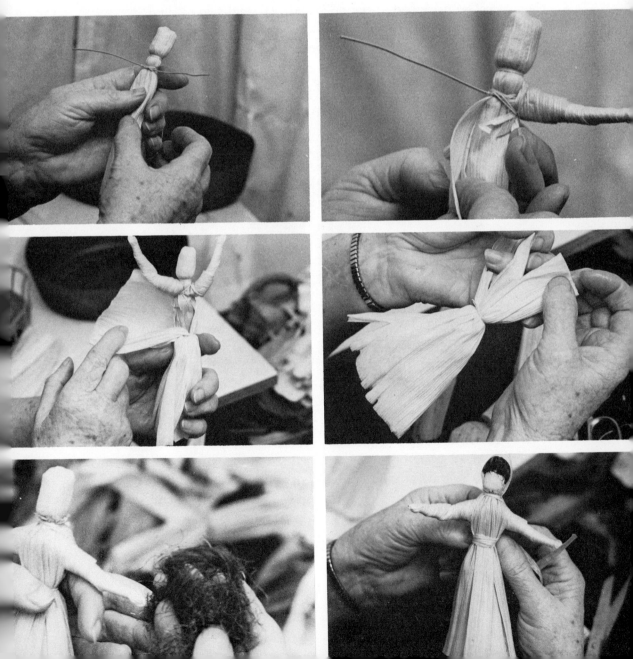

across the neck and under the armpit as you would to secure a bandage. Layers are added until the arms are properly thick. Then the feet are wrapped, continuing up the legs to the hips. The two wires are joined together above this point by wrapping the husks for the body around both. The body is tied with string at the hips, waist, and shoulders. The doll is now ready to be dressed.

The girl doll shown in the photographs was dressed relatively simply. First a husk was wrapped around the doll and tied at the waist. The upper part was folded down over the lower part to form a petticoat and skirt. A colored outer skirt could have been added and tied at the waist. Colored husks could then have been wrapped around the arms as sleeves. A full husk was then wrapped at the neck and tied, and tied again at the waist. The skirt was trimmed to proper length. She was given a sash made from a folded-over strip of husk tied in back.

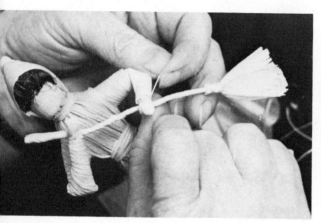 

The hair is made of corn silk which was placed across the head and over the face. A string was tied around the forehead and then the silk was flipped back and rolled on either side of the face. A corn husk kerchief was added and the doll was handed a broom made, of course, of corn husks. Black and red drawing ink and a fine-tipped pen were used for the facial features.

Lila Marshall also gave directions for clothing a male figure. Colored husks, wrapped around the arms and tied at the shoulders, form the sleeves of the shirt. Starting at the foot, husks of the desired color are wrapped to form the trousers and tied at the hips. Then a straight piece is cut for a shirt, the doll placed on it, and the strip wrapped around it with a slit on each side so that it can come around to the front, leaving the arms out.

Then it is tied at the neck. A strip the color of the pants is wrapped around the waist to cover the end of the shirt. The strip is brought down between the legs and tied in the back at the waistline. The coat is made like the shirt, but longer. A slit is made under each arm to bring it around to the front, where it is left open.

If made with firm wire and wrapped to just the right thickness, the dolls can be bent into virtually any position. If they are to stand up, the bottom of the leg wire should be looped, with the loop forming the foot and the end of the wire a spur pointing backward for support. They can be given brooms, churns, spinning wheels, pipes, jump ropes, tiny violins carved with a razor blade. They can ride corn husk horses or read miniature newspapers.

Lila Marshall suggests that people who are unable to gather their own husks can order them from a place in California which picks and prepares them properly for craft use—and for wrapping tamales. It's Mojave Foods Co., 958 Northeastern Avenue, Los Angeles, California 90063.

III ∿ OTHER TOYS AND MODELS

The toy-maker named Willard Watson comes from Deep Gap, North Carolina, not far from the town of Boone. His wife, Ora, is a fine quilter. Most of his carved wooden toys are intricately jointed creations which move in strange ways when propelled by a wiggle or a turn of a crank. Most are traditional Appalachian playthings; a few are totally original.

"This here fellow will do a dance," he says, demonstrating. "Some calls him limberjack, some calls him dancin' doll, and it doesn't matter— he'll answer either way."

The work shed is lavishly cluttered with wooden doll bodies and arm and leg pieces. They vary in color from white to dark brown. Some are cut from pine, some from cedar, others from black walnut. Completed dancing dolls may be fashioned from a single type of wood or from a combination of two or three. Watson shows how the joints are fitted together and then fastened with tiny nails to allow them to move freely. Mountain toy-makers have always favored such simple carved mechanical creations.

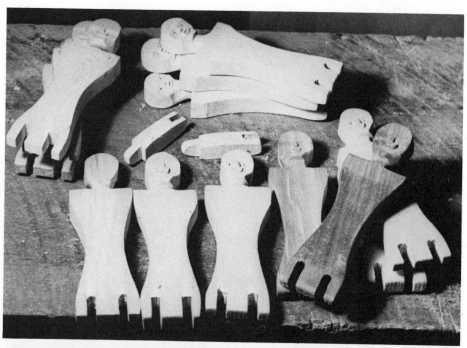

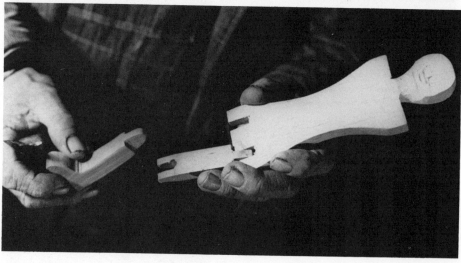

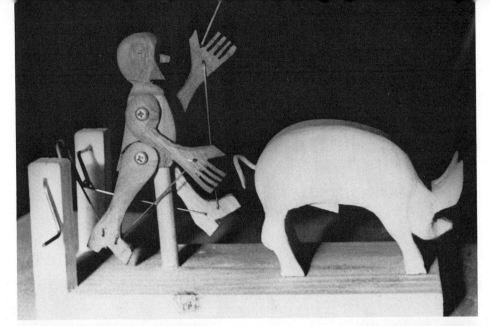

"Now this here I calls 'the kickin' pig.'" He turns the crank on a small platform which holds a man carved in black walnut and a pig carved in pine. Despite the title it is the man who kicks and not the pig. "When you turn it he kicks him and he whups him at the same time too," he says.

There are toys which don't perform and are more like intricate models. Two horses pull a covered wagon. A man holds the reins of a mule; "My daughter Pansy made the clothes for the man."

One popular figure is a rooster, which Watson carves from laurel. An appropriately sized, correctly branched piece of wood is cut from one of the large laurels which fill the woods near his house. The lower piece of the stem will be split to form two legs; the upper piece will become the head, and the branch will become the tail. The legs are whittled to a pleasing roundness. The head is simply carved, and then the tail feathers are shaved down one by one. It all looks deceptively simple as Watson cuts precisely regular pieces of laurel, leaving each attached at the end of the cut. "Though sometimes I drop a feather. Not often."

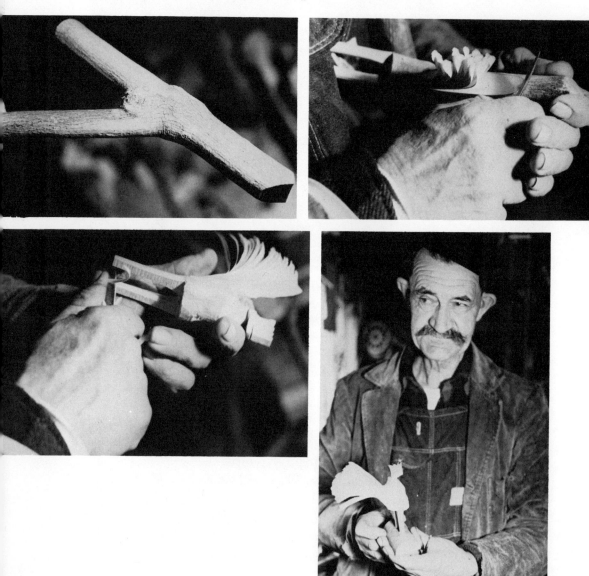

When all the feathers are cut he bends them into a graceful fan, touches the comb and gills with bright red paint, and sets the perky bird on another piece of wood. The rooster is carved green, and when the wood dries the feathers stay in place.

Laurel is also the wood Watson chooses for his powerful slingshots. He demonstrates his skill outside the shed. Stones ring out against selected distant targets. "We useter hunt squirrels with these here slingshots when I was a boy," he says. "They have to be first-rate rubber. First-rate. You just tie them with string. If hit breaks, well, tie it again!"

Watson's claim to distinction does not begin and end with woodcarving. He is proud to have been the man who set up a still and demonstrated its use "right in front of the United States capitol." The occasion was the Smithsonian Institution's annual Folklife Festival, and Watson was brought up from Deep Gap for this purpose. How does he really feel about the subject of home brew?

"It tastes a hundred times better than anythin' you buy," he says, closing the issue.

William Ledford is a man with a strong sense of history and regional pride. "I've lived in these mountains all my life," he explains, "and I've worked fixing up some of these old cabins. When I make my model cabins they're done just the way the old ones was made, with the same materials, but on a scale of one-half inch to the foot."

Ledford is an expert on the subject. "The poor people had little cabins with no windows. Later they left a hole and put in greased paper to get some light inside. They was made of poles—regular round logs. You just carved out a saddle notch on the bottom and set hit on the log underneath. Some pole cabins was chestnut but the big ones in this part of the state was mostly poplar, sometimes oak, sometimes buckeye. I been restoring some that's in a state park over near Cumberland Gap and there's a whole settlement being saved. I got interested and started making models of different types."

His most recent model rests on a kitchen table. "This here model is of a real fancy cabin of squared-off poplar logs which would have been about six inches thick. The way they're fitted at the end is called a half dovetail."

He finds some small-scale pieces—"Here's two that's afittin' good"—and shows the method of cutting and construction. "This here model is of a big cabin—thirty-two by twenty-two feet—with a fine stone chimbley and a roof made of red oak shakes. Of course there was no mills in those days and everythin' was hand-cut. See the boards under the gable end of the roof? That's the kind I seen on the old cabins. I chinked the cabin with clay like they did then. Almost everyone used clay but some of the wealthy people had lime kilns and they mixed the lime and sand for mortar to chink the cabin."

Homer Miracle, along with his versatile wife, son, and daughter, keeps his shop, Miracle's Mountain Crafts, supplied with all sorts of homemade items for sale. The small store is located in a modest frame structure on a highway outside Middlesboro, Kentucky—a town which borders the Kentucky entrance to Cumberland Gap National Park. The surrounding woods and fields supply the Miracles with just about every raw material they need: wood for chairs and carvings and dough bowls, broomcorn for brooms, corn husks for artificial flowers and dolls, apples for Mrs. Miracle's apple-faced dolls, and a seed named "Judas's tears," which she inserts for their eyes.

Elm and hickory bark are stripped for weaving chair seats when the sap is highest. The Miracles prefer to do it at the new moon in June.

"First you cut down the tree," son James K. Miracle explains. "Then you take off the dead outer part of the bark with a drawing knife. Then you go down the length of the tree with a knife and cut grooves and strip off the inner bark. Then you just weave your seat. The bark is rough at first, but the seat of your pants will wear it down real quick. The little doll chairs is made just like the big ones."

Homer Miracle is a former miner, in poor health, who sits by the coal stove whittling finely constructed miniature ladder-back chairs for the dolls made by his wife. The dolls sell well, and the chairs are precisely constructed. He likes using birch sticks whittled from split blocks of the wood. "We call it river or water birch," he says. "This kind of wood, when it's green you can bend it with your thumb. See how I do it? I just use my pocket knife. I whittle the ladders, bend them, and put them in a brace. Then I make holes in the posts and down in the ladders. Then I put together the front part, the rounds which connect the front to the back, and get it all together. The rockers go on next and then the arms and then I weave a seat from bark or cane, just like the seats on the big chairs." The doll chairs are perfect in all details. "My father was a carpenter and a blacksmith and we're still usin' all his tools."

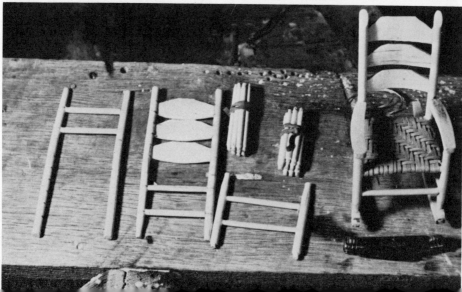

DECORATIVE ARTS

IV ∽ WOODCARVING

Edgar Tolson lives in the town of Campton, Kentucky, population 640 souls. He is a tall, lean man with a jutting jaw, a former carpenter and the father of fourteen children. Following a serious illness in middle age he left his vocation, took up his whittling knife, and began to carve the farm animals he knew—and then, with particular fascination, various species of wildlife he had never seen. When he later turned to the human form his imagination continued to be stirred by the exotic. He has carved Indian maidens, Uncle Sam, Adam and Eve in the Garden. His men and women stand erect and gaze back at the viewer with an unblinking assurance.

At first Edgar Tolson simply gave his carvings away to friends, but now they are bought by folklorists, crafts connoisseurs, artists, and nonartists who find in Tolson's self-taught primitive style of woodcarving an engaging charm, humor, and genuine aesthetic significance. He once did a complete Noah's Ark but he sold it years ago to someone who lives far from the confines of this eastern Kentucky small town.

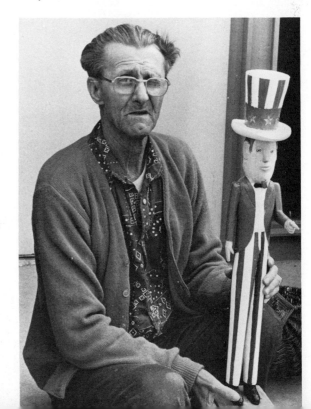

How is it done? "With a penknife, this here rasp, and some sandpaper." He shows some of his earlier animal carvings, two yoked oxen and a small elephant with ears on the alert. "Hit took me the longest time to learn how to carve eyes. See these here? Them eyes is just pegs. I made a little hole and drove 'em in. Then later I learned to *cut* the eye in. There's two things you have to do. First you carve the lid and when that's done you carve in the sight."

One of his works in progress is a mountain lion whose form is beginning to emerge from a small rectangular block of poplar measuring 2-½ by 2-½ by 5 inches. "On animals the way you work is, you start on the flat end with the face. You always start with the face; first the ears, and then you come down here like this, and you dress the nose down the way you want it, thisaway. It's all square, a lion's face. The only thing in doing the whole animal is, you got to have in your mind all the time the shape of the lion."

He is also working on a unicorn. The legs will later be carved separately and glued to the body. "I never seen a unicorn, did you? They hain't got them in this part of the country, but a girl sent me a picture from a tapestry in the Metropolitan Museum in New York so I decided to try and make one. They're sure peculiar. They got a nose way up here and a chin beard like a goat only different because one part curls back thisaway and two go *this*away. I'm goin' to carve that beard with the three curls and then make a little dowel at the end and a hole in the chin and glue it in there."

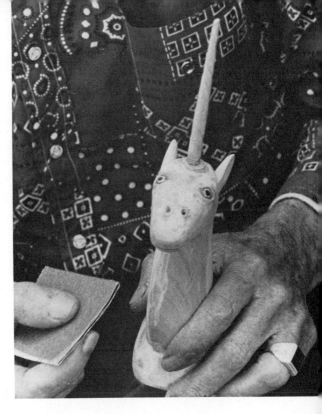

The wood Tolson prefers to use is poplar, because he finds it the best carving wood available. "Buckeye is good. Hit grows over in Breathitt County but not as I can get at. I use cedar for the apples when I do Adam and Eve because of the color. The snake is outa poplar but I paint him black because that's what he was—a blacksnake."

Adam and Eve are also carved from rectangular blocks but Tolson

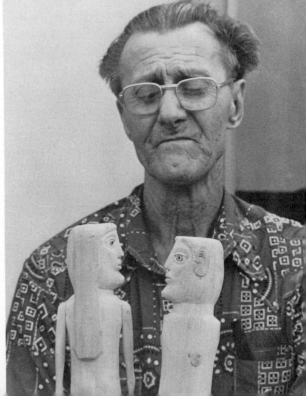

cautions on how to begin. "For people you start the face on a corner of the wood, never on the flat side. I used to carve them with the arms on but that way you're workin' the splittin' way and that's not good. Now I carve them separately, with the grain, and then I glue them on."

He shows an incomplete Adam and Eve and the beginning of a tree. The lower tree limbs will be carved and attached later, as will the apples. Another roughed-out Adam and Eve face sideways. "Adam hain't got his arms on yet," he apologizes. "This is Eve. She's alookin' back goin' out of the garden and there will be an angel with a sword in his hand and closest to him the tree. They're not like the other pair. They're on the way out, alookin' back, and they done dropped their apples."

Tolson has suffered many recent problems—with his health, a difficult change of residence, the loss of his few tools to a thief. But he hopes to finish the new figures soon. "I wanted to do one of them for my daughter for Christmas because she asked for it. My doctor collects my things," he says proudly. "He has them in a case in the waitin' room. He wouldn't sell them to nobody for no amount."

Drive to the city of Cumberland, Maryland; continue through the mountains and then turn toward the West Virginia border, go through the village, zig and zag a bit past a brick Methodist church. Around the curve you will come to the trim house and manicured garden of Mr. and Mrs. Claude Yoder.

Yoder is one of the most common names among the Mennonites of Garrett County. Claude Yoder—proud of his heritage—talks about his childhood. "I grew up twenty miles west of here in Grantsville," he says. "We little Dutch boys used to swim in the river there under that old stone bridge." When Yoder was a boy the Mennonites of western Maryland kept pretty much "to our own kind," he explains, and they still do today. "There's a good many Mennonites and also Amish down here. Some people think Mennonite and Amish are the same!" he says in amazement.

He takes out a framed newspaper article several decades old, about Mrs. Yoder's father—she was a Schrock—who lived to be one hundred. Past generations of Yoders and Schrocks were farmers in these lush hills in the extreme western part of Maryland, strangely shaped on the map—wedged between Pennsylvania and West Virginia. Claude Yoder, however, worked most of his adult life at the Celanese plant in Cresaptown. "I missed three days of work in thirty-three years," he tells the visitors. His son, whose paintings are displayed throughout the house, is a professional art teacher.

Yoder is a self-taught woodcarver, and now that he's retired he is able to devote full time to what has always been his most compelling interest.

An awesome figure of an eagle rests heavily on a large stump. Its powerful wings are unfurled and its head stretches back and up, at once vulnerable and menacing. The marks of the woodcarving gouge are strong and sure. It somehow seems incongruous that this polite and pious, cheerful, and scrubbed-looking man conceived and executed the fierce figure of the predator.

"I went to get fireplace wood from a man who had some to get rid of and I saw this—I think it's ash—and the way it was, it was a piece of a thick trunk that branched out like this, like a Y." He shows how the wings of the bird stretch up and outward. "So I said to the man, 'I want that piece of wood,' and he said, 'You don't want that. It won't even fit in the fireplace!'" Yoder chuckles. "So I brought it home and I carved the eagle. I thought and thought on it, whether to round out the bottom or leave it part of the trunk, and I think I did it the best way."

Many people want to buy the bird, but it's not for sale. It is displayed out in the garden. Will it survive?

"I put a plastic over him when it's real wet but he's all right. He'll weather, I expect. He'll last as long as Claude will, that's certain."

The large garden is filled with bird feeders, and Yoder is an avid bird watcher. He walks in the woods looking for pieces of wood, tangled roots, and old logs. He has a keen eye for decayed and weathered branches that will make interesting bases, an attentive ear for birds flying overhead.

On shelves in the house he has others of his carvings—small figures of men and women, animals, Amish farmers, a biblical-looking shepherd, a horse pulling a cart, an old man with a pipe. They are "folky" and crude and charming.

The birds are his triumph. Some are mounted on pieces of driftwood. Others simply stand on the uncarved lower part of tree trunks. A hawk looks imperiously down at the viewer. "A neighbor hauled this piece of Ponderosa pine all the way from Utah. What nice neighbors I have. I made

this hawk from it. Real nice wood for carving. No, I couldn't sell that. You see, my neighbor gave me the wood. It wouldn't be right."

Another grand eagle, about three feet tall, holds its head high. Yoder thinks the material is basswood but he's not certain. The bird is poised, listening, tense, proud—ready to unfurl its wings with a thundering sound. The snow owls are quiet. They stand by the fireplace and their eyes are black and innocent. Yoder carved them from white birch which another friend brought him from Canada. "I'd like to plant some of those birches. It's something I've been wanting to do for a long time. I just don't know if they'd grow the same here. The wood is naturally white, just like this." He has left the surface of the owls rough, after a coarse rasp has removed the marks of the gouge and the chisel.

Claude Yoder hasn't any strong preferences when it comes to wood. "I like them all. I like carving walnut and butternut, sugar maple and cherry and apple. Sometimes I use a little stain, like on the wings of this eagle, and sometimes just boiled linseed oil and sometimes nothing."

In the basement there is a workbench and an immense old butcher's block made from a tree trunk to which he has attached a vise. He has been carving down on the block hour after hour, year after year. "To tell the truth, I never had one bird I was really satisfied with. I don't like them half as much up here as I did in the basement when I was working on them."

Mrs. Yoder, who is baking bread, is embarrassed by the clutter of tools and chips and shavings. "Oh, don't go down there," she cries in mock horror from her impeccable kitchen. Her husband leads the way down the stairs.

"It's a lot of satisfaction working with wood," he says. "It takes a good bit of time to make a piece you like and then sometimes you work and work and it's never right." He chuckles. "I feel like if you have a boy with a lot of patience and not too much upstairs the best thing is to make a whittler out of him."

The Spiker brothers—Charlie, George, and Lonny—live up a hollow near Grantsville, Maryland, in a place called Meadow Mountain. The three old men—a fourth brother died recently—raise rabbits, tend small vegetable patches, and do some woodcarving. The hollow isn't visible from the main road, and although this is unusual in rural communities, it's difficult to locate anyone in the vicinity who can give directions. The Spiker brothers are reclusive. The road into their land is impassable by car. People who live half a mile away don't rightly know how you'd get there. "It's somewhere back in the mountain. Don't try to drive in there. Best to walk."

The brothers refer to their narrow shadowy hollow as "the old home place." It's where they were raised, although the actual house they were born in burned down years ago. Each brother has built himself a cabin. Charlie's is made of logs with bits of tar paper nailed over the cracks instead of chinking. George and Lonny have built their homes out of pieces of this and that—tar paper, some asphalt shingles, a bit of wood, some sheetrock, some roofing material, a few logs, heavy vinyl-coated paper with a harlequin pattern. All the brothers keep barking dogs that announce visitors with fearful yelps.

Charlie, who is planting beans in his garden, is a sweet-faced chatty man. "I left home about fourteen and worked on the railroad. Later I was an engineer riding from Akron to Chicago. I was onct in Floridy. That's the coming place, you know. When I retired I come back to the old home place. I like to whittle things and done a bit of carving, though I can't see good at night. My daddy, he whittled some and he made all the axe handles and pick handles with his whittlin' knife."

Charlie walks out toward the woods and points out a small plant growing close to a rock. "This here is ginseng. Folks'll pay big money for it. They sell it to China. They smoke it out there and they make medicines. It's said to keep you young. I dig it out from the woods and plant it here where I can watch it and then I get the berries and plant more. A fella from Pennsylvania pays me big money for it. This here is another good plant but not worth money. You call it black cohash. The Indians named it and folks make poultices from it.

"I sell some of my rabbits that I don't eat. I sell some of my whittlin' too up at the craft shop, but not much. I made this fork and spoon after a picture I saw of some whittlin' from Africa. I make a lot of these letter openers and some of these little men and some animals. Then I do arrows. Things like that. That kind of thing."

Lonny is reputed to be very shy, and at first he doesn't want to talk about himself, but then he changes his mind. He's working on a small interlocking wooden puzzle. "My daddy used to make these. This is the old home place but all is left of the house is the chimbley."

Lonny has worked at various times in the nearby sawmill and before that in the coal mines. He was in the army during World War II. "I hain't traveled much away from the old home place since I got out of the army in 1943."

With a small smile he brings out a wooden puzzle toy. A T-shaped bar has been carved so that balls, originally part of the same piece of wood, roll back and forth in channels. "People ask, 'How do you get the ball out?' Well, you *cain't* get the ball out —that's the thing about it." Lonny also carves the one-piece wooden chains that are the pride of many skilled Appalachian whittlers. "For a chain you use butternut. You have to

use a right sharp knife and keep turnin' and turnin'. This here chain, I did two links and it broke. I have the artheritis in my fingers and can't see good but it's still an interesting thing to do."

He brings out a handful of round dust-colored pebbles that he's picked up and saved. They look like balls of clay and each has some rough suggestion of facial features. "There's a whole lot interesting in the country. See the face in this pebble? The water made it. See this one? It's like an old man 'cept no mouth on it and 'cept only one eye but a right good ear. You have to look at it sharp."

George Spiker is almost totally blind now and very deaf. He doesn't carve his animals anymore, but sometimes he picks at one with his knife. He

is standing out by the shed near one of the rabbit hutches trying to smooth out the place behind the wooden pig's ear that was never quite right. "This is the old home place, you know," he says in a frail hoarse voice. The fine little pig has cobwebs between its legs.

V ∽ SNAKE CANES, WOODEN AND CORN HUSK FLOWERS, AND COAL CRAFT

Listening to Robert Lipe talk, you would never guess that he is a practitioner of one of Appalachia's most unusual decorative arts. "On a nice day there's nothin' I like better than goin' out to hunt snakes in the woods. I hunt snakes the way some hunts rabbits." The most passionate humanitarians could not find fault with the hunting of Robert Lipe. The "snakes" he seeks are botanical, not zoological specimens. Lipe, known to many crafts enthusiasts as "the snake cane carver," makes remarkable walking sticks from young tree trunks which have put forth bark and wood in a curious fashion in response to the tightening pressures of vines. The result is a cane which is more decorative than utilitarian—not to be confused with the sturdy walking sticks whittled by others.

"What happens is, the vine grows around the tree or bush. It's usually honeysuckle or smoke vine or wild grape, and what happens is, it chokes the tree. Then the tree sets to growin' out around the vine. The vine always grows around the tree to the left. It's because of the way the earth turns when the sun goes around. The vine reaches towards the sun when it's growin'."

A collection of uncarved, freshly cut snakes rests against a tree in Lipe's back yard. Some are thick, some thin. Most are sassafras but there are other types of wood as well.

"I've had 'em grow around oak, sycamore, sourwood, sumac. They don't grow much around pine. I cut them in October or November up through about the middle of March. After that the sap comes up and if you cut them in spring or summer the bark won't stay on. A lot of them

are crooked and I have to put 'em in a vise until they season out. It's easier if the wood is green. If they're dead I put 'em in water overnight and then set 'em in the vise while they're wet so they won't break."

Mrs. Lipe comes out to join the discussion. "He'd rather carve those canes than eat," she says cheerfully, and certainly his enthusiasm for the subject is obvious. There are snake canes everywhere—propped against the hedge, against a door, filling an old baking powder barrel.

His method of transforming a deformed tree trunk into a handsome and remarkable walking stick is basically simple. He whittles the outer and inner bark from the straight part of the tree trunk. Then he works more delicately on the extra wood that covers the vine and forms the snake to emphasize the shape, which is precisely like that of a reptile wrapping itself around a stick. He shapes the "head," the thickest part of the woody overgrowth; sets beads in for eyes; and fashions a flexible tongue from rubber bands, which are glued into a slit mouth. He removes all parts of the bark that would flake or peel off, carefully leaving whatever he can to create the effect of reptile skin. The finished cane is actually turned upside down, so the thicker lower part of the tree becomes the upper part of the walking stick.

The canes, when completed, are amazingly varied in shape and color. Some are heavy powerful-looking snakes; others are long and narrow; some are gray, some a protective green or brown, and others are coppery. They form a virtual snake zoo and seem almost scientifically identifiable.

"My daddy used to make them when I was a boy," Lipe says. "When I retired from house-building I got into this to have something to do. Some is more snake-faced than others, and you never know looking at them exactly what color they'll turn out to be. I try not to make them too much alike. Sometimes I varnish them when they're finished, sometimes I don't. Sometimes when you take the bark off it leaves the snake all speckledy. This one out of persimmon is more like a snake than any I ever saw.

"First thing, I take the vine out and rub around with sandpaper. If there's big spaces I fill in where the vine was, or where the wood was rotten, with Plastic Wood. Then I sand the stick part real good. Sometimes I cut away the stick and have just the snake turning round and round."

Mr. and Mrs. Lipe live in Rogersville, Tennessee, in the northeastern part of the state. He sells his canes at the flea market in Kingsport. Their pleasant farmhouse is sited in a grassy valley near the foot of a strange mountain peak which rises to a sharp unlikely point.

"We call it 'Devil's Nose,'" says Mrs. Lipe. "When we were children we used to hide Easter eggs there. I bet some are still there, those Easter eggs."

"And plenty of good snakes," adds her husband. "It's such a nice day, I think I'll go out and hunt me some more. Anybody want to come?"

His wife bustles toward the house to chat with the parson's wife, who

has stopped by for a visit. She looks back over her shoulder and shakes her head. "That man would rather make his canes than *eat*."

A rose is a rose is a rose, but in Appalachia it just might be corn husks instead. And watch out for those daisies, zinnias, chrysanthemums, because skilled whittlers are at work all through these hills simulating them in hickory, walnut, and cedar.

These artificial flowers do not, of course, fool the eye, but they have an appeal entirely lacking in manufactured artificial flowers. Plastic can only be plastic, but a shaved-wood zinnia is a triumph of ingenuity in the use of natural materials. There is really no mystery about the delight of seeing raw materials which have been picked in the fields and gathered in the woods transformed into something unexpected and beautiful. The fact that the flowers are purely decorative means that they lack the added interest of function, but their charm is undeniable.

Mrs. Hazel Miracle and her daughter Janice are both experts at making flowers. They sell them at the family shop, Miracle Mountain Crafts, in southeastern Kentucky. It is not difficult to learn Janice's method of fashioning corn husk roses, although it involves some trial and error. It is quite another matter to learn to shave wooden flowers so that the petals are thin and delicate, equal in size, yet firmly attached at the base. Mrs. Miracle makes it look simple. Neither Janice nor her brother James, both skilled at numerous crafts, has been able to develop the skill.

Hazel Miracle begins with a hickory stick about six inches long that has been split from a log and whittled into a correct thickness and even roundness. It will make a cream-colored flower. If she wants white flowers she uses maple. Basswood—also known as linden—will make a beige flower; cedar gives a warm russet color, and walnut flowers are a dark brown. Mrs. Miracle makes them all but advises that hickory is the easiest wood to use and therefore the best type for beginners. The six-inch stick will actually make several flowers. She uses only the last inch and a half of the stick for each flower.

She begins whittling petals, stopping just at the right point. Go a fraction farther with the knife and the petal will float to the ground. She keeps rotating the stick with her left hand as she works around the stick in rows. Each row of petals stops a fraction higher than the last. The shavings curl outward as they're cut. She keeps circling until the end of the stick is as thin as the point of a pencil, and then she breaks it off and the flower is

complete. The end of the stick is then cut off straight and another flower can be started. The point at which the flower was broken off becomes the center of the blossom. The flat end becomes the bottom. A small hole is drilled and a small stick or reed is inserted as a stem.

Mrs. Miracle's dogwood flowers are an original design she conceived some years ago. "I saw something like it on a quilt once," she says, "and I thought I could do it with the shavin's Homer and James was makin' with all their woodworkin'."

The flowers are almost lifelike. Mrs. Miracle makes them by first cutting the thin shavings into squares and then into petal-shaped pieces with her scissors. "Then when my boy is makin' stools I say, 'Cut me some of them

buttons.' That's what I call them—buttons. You see they're just little round pieces of wood, like a button or a dime. What I do is, I put some glue on the bottom and stick the petals on. The center, it's just sawdust. We don't throw nothin' away here! I put a drop of glue in the middle and put on the dust and blow off what's extra. The greenish yellow center is painted, and I paint the tip of the petals like they are when they grow. Then I drill a little hole in the bottom of the button and I pick me some thin, branchy pieces of bamboo cane down by the river—we call it fishin' cane—and put one flower on each branch so it's just like a sprig you cut from a tree in the woods."

Janice Miracle's corn husk roses, thickly bunched in a large crock, bloom year round in a cheerful profusion. Janice makes her roses in three hues. Some are red; others are yellow; still others are made with undyed husks, and their crisp parchmentlike quality makes them the most interesting of all. The husks are gathered, as they are for doll-making, after the corn is fully mature and past the eating stage. They are carefully smoothed and dried for storage so that they won't mildew.

To start a flower she first cuts the dry husks with scissors into large heart-shaped pieces. If she is going to make red or yellow flowers she then dyes the husks and permits them to dry. Using a whittled-down hickory stick or a long reed for a stem, she makes a small tight knob for a bud, using the tops of the corn husks left from the petal cutting and tying them securely at the base. The tip of each petal must be quickly moistened and then curled around a finger before being added so that it will bend in the desired direction.

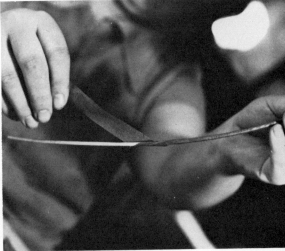

When the rose is sufficiently layered with petals more string is tied to keep them securely rooted at the base. Husks which have been dyed green are cut with a feathery edge to cover the base of the flower. They must completely conceal the string. When they are in place Janice holds them with one hand and tapes them to the stem with green florist's tape. She then continues to wind the tape around the reed, working down until the reed is completely covered and becomes a green stem.

Most people think of wood, clay, and plant products when the term "natural materials" is used in connection with crafts. To West Virginians this classification also includes the most commonplace of natural materials—coal. A number of people in the state have turned an interest in whittling into skill in carving coal.

Michael Pegram of Beckley, West Virginia, about fifty miles south of Charleston, uses the local bituminous and cannel coal for carving and casting figures. He plans to build a small shop out of large lumps of coal put together with mortar.

His best-selling figures are a miner and a sitting black bear. First the figure is carved out of coal with a penknife. Then Pegram makes a rubber mold for casting. "You just can't get your money back if you carve all of them—it's too time-consuming." He shows some coal ground "just as fine as face powder," which he will mix with a polyester resin as a combining agent and pour into the molds.

In addition to the figures, Pegram makes pen sets and a large range of jewelry items.

DOMESTIC ARTS

VI ∽ HOUSEHOLD WOODENWARE, CHAIRS, BIRD HOUSES, AND BROOMS

Making useful household objects out of wood is a craft that seems almost second nature to mountain men. Look beneath or alongside the benches on any street in an Appalachian town and you'll find piles of shavings left from the incessant whittling that accompanies good conversation. All Appalachian men carry penknives and most use them skillfully. Great respect has always been accorded to the man who, with outstanding ability, could notch logs for a cabin; put together a tight barrel for the home brew; make a firm rocker or a good bowl, a churn, a tool handle, wooden kitchen utensils.

The early settlers used wood for their homes and for virtually everything in them. Today's Appalachian woodworkers still employ simple tools and old techniques. The wood they like working with best is the wood that grows behind the house, up the mountain, and down the hollow: oak, hickory, maple, walnut, apple, cherry, linden, sassafras, cedar, buckeye, pine.

"Buckeye is the first choice for a bread tray, that's the best," says James K. Miracle, a burly young man who wields a heavy old tool called a howel with accuracy and enthusiasm. "The white type I like most. That's the smooth-barked type and it has the tightest grain. Yellow buckeye is what some folks calls the horse chestnut. I'd say the second choice was basswood—that's what you sometimes call linden. The third choice would be a yellow poplar."

James and his sister work with their mother and father making a variety of crafts objects in their shop. He makes miniature chairs for his mother's apple-faced dolls, carved wooden animals, bowls. He weaves chair seats from bark and can repair just about anything. The shop is filled with shavings and the woods behind it are rich with fine timber.

"You start by finding you a tree that's no more than twelve or fourteen inches down at the bottom. You cut it down and you should be able to get you a good many blocks from it, each one about thirty inches long. Then all you got to do is split the block down the middle. Each half of that block will make a good twenty-seven-inch-long bowl. You have to cut the buckeye in the winter or it will turn real blue color because of the sap." He shows a partially carved wooden bowl, one end of which is distinctly and strangely blue.

He lines up three bowls in various stages of completion. "The buckeye bowl will weigh about four to five pounds but in poplar it's going to weigh about three times as much. We call it a bread bowl or a dough bowl.

"The mountaineers in the old days used to make them and bring them down to the river and put white sand in them and scrub them with a rock to get them white and smooth. They used them mostly to let bread raise in. Now you don't know what people will use 'em for, so at the end, after it's all smoothed with sandpaper, I put on beeswax so it won't absorb odors."

James uses the tools his grandfather handed down. "These was old even then when he used 'em. A blacksmith in these parts made these tools a hundred and sixty years ago. They're iron with steel welded in at the cuttin' end. Axes are made the same way. My granddaddy was a blacksmith and a woodworker. He operated a sawmill. He could do just about everything."

Solomon Saylor, aged eighty-five, is known for his skill as a hunter; his five Kentucky rifles and one pistol ("for shootin' snakes") are kept in a rack over his bed—except when he's toting one up the hollow and into the woods. He is also known as a maker of the traditional mountain chair—a ladder-back straight chair, more precisely described as a mule-eared slat-back.

Saylor has been making chairs the same way all his life. "That's the way they're *supposed* to be made," he explains. First comes the frame, cut from hard maple, and then the "rounds" or rungs. He cuts those from oak or mulberry. He chops down trees "up the holler" and carries the wood back to his shed.

There are secrets to be kept by a Kentucky mountaineer who knows how

to make a good chair, and Saylor is a reticent man. He makes it all look simple, despite the fact that he uses only a few tools. He has an ingenious primitive wooden vise which holds a piece of wood in place while he works.

How does he make a "round" round? "With this here drawing knife." He shows how he works with the two-handled plane. He then dowels the ends with a penknife. "Mark it back about an inch and then just trim it down." He fits the rungs into holes cut with a brace and bit. "The back rounds go straight and the side ones out like this." He points out the fact that the chair is wider in front than in back. "That's the way they're made here. Just make your pieces and put 'em together," he says.

The chair of the pioneers was made in the same fashion, without glue or nails. The method is this. The posts are made from green wood and the

rungs and slats from thoroughly dried wood. They are fitted together, and as the posts dry their holes shrink and close in firmly over the doweled slats and rungs.

The next step is weaving a seat. Mr. Saylor manages that in no time at all with wood splits or the inner bark of the hickory tree or just about anything else that's handy.

What does he do next?

"Set down and talk awhile."

If you drive north and east from Kingsport, Tennessee, for about fifteen minutes, and head toward Hiltons, Virginia, and then take a left over by the river just before the bridge, and follow the river up awhile, you will

come to the tiny tidy white clapboard house of Mr. and Mrs. Louis Smallwood and their aged dachshund, Timmie.

The Holston River once sparkled but now it's polluted with mining waste. The fish cannot be eaten. The Smallwoods' rowboat bobs at the edge, tied to a tree. Timmie roots in the vegetable garden and mucks up the house and barks at the robins, under the adoring eyes of his master and mistress.

"He loves that dog more than he loves me," says Nannie Smallwood, a breathless animated lady.

"That's right," says Louis Smallwood, deadpan.

He is a man who looks like his name—short and slight, quiet and gentle. He doesn't laugh at his own jokes. His hearing is poor and his wife cautions, "You have to talk loud to him. He can hear *me*. Honey. HONEY! Show them your bowl."

The work shed is behind the house. The bowl is a fine traditional scooped dough bowl. Small useful and decorative buckets, cedar bowls, and churns fill the work shed and the house. "Show them your chain," shouts Nannie Smallwood, and he exhibits a technical triumph of woodcarving—a chain made from a single stick of wood. "He likes for me to suggest," says Mrs. Smallwood. "I suggest and he makes."

Mr. Smallwood's wooden bowls are for sale, but not the banjo he made her recently, just for fun. She steps out to the front of the house by the river to show that it can be played as well as admired. The banjo is made entirely of wood with no skin whatsoever. The sides and neck are cedar and it has a copper rim. It is made precisely the way the sides of the cedar buckets are fashioned. "Hit sounds real good," says Mrs. Smallwood. She looks about nervously. "Where is the baby?" Timmie is barking at a tall weed. "Oh, there he is."

Smallwood learned his woodworking methods from his father, a maker of cedar buckets. "He takes these pieces of wood, just as rough as stove wood, and he puts them one after another side by side and puts them in a rim."

"No glue," says Smallwood.

"He don't use no glue," Mrs. Smallwood interprets.

"First the old rim."

"First he puts them in the old rim when they're green and then he lets them season all bent in a circle like that. How long, honey? They want to know how long do they season."

"Two weeks."

"Two weeks. Then he smooths out the outside and carves out the inside smooth and takes off that old band and they're all bent in a circle with no glue or nails. Then he puts on a good rim of brass or copper."

She fetches a group of fine little buckets with lids and bases. A lidless model filled with fruit stands in the center of her kitchen table. "Hit takes a long time. When he sells a churn I figure he makes about twenty cents an hour, but he likes doing it. He's real old-timey."

When asked about tools, Mr. Smallwood takes a cigar box and a saw from his workshop. "These is all the tools I got," he says.

"That's all," Nannie Smallwood chirps. "He's real old-timey. I like things more modern. My favorite love is Elvis Presley. I have ideas, so I suggest and he makes."

There are all sorts of household items beautifully fashioned by Mr.

Smallwood's penknife. Some, like the rolling pin and the brooms, are useful. Others, like the wooden scissors, are ornamental—a display of skill, a piece of work done for no purpose other than the delight of creating it.

A number of traditional crafts of the southern Appalachian region are highly refined and complex, and only craftsmen who possess unusual abilities undertake them. Among the most interesting hand-crafted items, however, are workaday objects of a beautiful simplicity which have been made by generation after generation of mountain men because they serve a useful function in the house or on the farm. Many of these ingenious prod-

ucts, such as gourd bird houses and hickory scrub brooms, are made of one material, which you acquire by going out behind the house and picking it or cutting it from a tree.

Mr. Smallwood makes bird houses from the long-necked gourds he grows by the shed. Like many other Appalachian farmers, he hangs them in clusters from trees near his vegetable patch. The bird houses attract martins, he says, which in turn repay the favor by destroying insects that damage the crops. Here is an example of organic pest control at its most efficient.

The gourds are picked in October when they ripen and are left to hang in the barn and dry out for at least ninety days. The construction of the bird house takes a few minutes. Simply cut a small round hole, shake out the dried pulp and seeds, and eureka—a house any martin would be proud to claim!

If you cut a bigger hole in the gourd you have a dipper to use at the well. Lop off the long neck and scoop it out and glue on some wooden feet and you have a fine bowl. If you're as skillful as Louis Smallwood you can also carve a wooden lid.

Broom-making is another of Mr. Smallwood's diversified talents. Broomcorn grows in the field. "Just break it down, let it dry, scrape the seeds off, put it in warm water till it's soft, and tie it to the stick."

"I never *ever* paid money to buy a broom," says Nannie Smallwood. "My mamma used to wash our cabin floor with a broom just like this one." She brings out a different type of broom—an Appalachian hickory scrub broom, whittled from a strong straight hickory limb. Mr. Smallwood has been making them all his life. "When I was a child we didn't have no soap or detergent or anything we have today," his wife explains. "My mamma used to beat one rock with a bigger one until she had a bowlful of sand, then she spread it out on the wooden floor and wetted a scrub broom like this one and began to scrub. I tell you, the floor was just as white and clean as a plate."

The broom is worked green, and the stick must be a good straight one with no knots in it. It's not as easy as it looks to whittle the shavings so

they are thin yet substantial. It takes a good soaking to make them pliable enough to be bent down in correct position. A piece of wire or bark is then twisted around the broom to keep it firmly in scrub broom shape.

It is getting late and Mr. Smallwood has nothing else to show. Mrs. Smallwood offers to give a demonstration of Appalachian step dancing. She puts on a warped scratched record and begins to dance as Timmie destroys a newspaper. Everyone has coffee.

"Come again. Come back real soon. You remember how to get back. Just foller the river."

VII ~ BASKETS AND POTTERY

Two types of containers were available to the Appalachian pioneers: baskets and clay crocks. Good-quality native clay was plentiful, as were basket-making materials—wood "splits," grasses, reeds, vines, and small willow branches.

In early times, and until comparatively recently, baskets were used by all mountain people for storing, for gathering, for carrying items to and from market. Special shapes and sizes and weaves were devised for particular purposes. Closely woven baskets were used to hold seeds and ground meal and to measure grain. A loosely woven animal carrier with a small handle was especially designed for bringing live chickens from farm to market.

All sorts of trees, bushes, and weeds have been used in the mountains for basket-making. Broomcorn has been used, as have corn husks. Long pine needles are commonly woven into baskets near the coastal area of South Carolina. Ash splits were the favorite material in the northern Appalachians, particularly suitable for the famous Adirondack ash pack baskets.

Archaeologists say that the eastern band of the Cherokees were skilled basket-makers hundreds of years ago, and surely the early settlers must have studied their products and been strongly influenced by their designs and selection of materials. What remains of the old baskets is impressions left in clay surfaces, many of them remarkably sharp. It is known that when the explorer de Soto came through these parts in 1540 he wrote home praising the Cherokee baskets. Those with wide tops were used for storing and gathering, those with narrow tops were used for catching fish. A woven sifter was used in pounding meal to desired fineness.

The Cherokees traditionally dye their basket-making materials. To make their dyes they use boiled walnut root for black or dark brown, puccoon root for red, and other dyes made from berries, roots, leaves, hulls, flowers,

fruits, and seeds. These highly decorative baskets were photographed at
the Qualla Gift Shop in Cherokee, North Carolina. They were made by
Cherokee Indians on the reservation adjoining Great Smoky Mountains
National Park, from bark, white oak and maple splits, honeysuckle, and
river cane.

Among mountain men and women basket-making has always been an
ideal home craft because so few tools and materials are used and because
baskets are light and cheaply made. A scattering of basket-makers who
know the old techniques can be found today in all parts of the Appalachians.

Mr. and Mrs. William Cook, white oak basket makers, enjoy speculating
on the origins of their craft. Mr. Cook feels certain that the Indians of
pioneer days learned to make his type of baskets from the settlers. "They
probably taught the settlers how to weave baskets with reeds and grasses
and things they could pick. But they didn't have nothin' to cut down the
trees with, so they couldn't have made them from wood splits."

The Cooks live in Luray, Virginia, near the famous prehistoric caverns
and the northern limits of the skyline drive. Their ancestors lived in the
same region.

"I was born and raised right over thar on that next mountain. The farm
was so steep the chickens used to fall down the hill and kill theirselves!"
The basket-maker laughs, pointing out the window of the work shed behind
his house where he and his wife have been making baskets for forty-eight
years.

His full name is William Cody Cook, named after Buffalo Bill by his older brother—"They was alookin' for a name." His wife is Lucy. He's left-handed and she's right-handed, which is a great asset in their line of work. "Usually I weave the bottom of the basket," he explains, "and then I give it her and she weaves the sides." He demonstrates the fact that a left-handed basket-maker weaves in a counterclockwise direction and a right-handed person weaves clockwise. The bottom of the basket is worked from the inside, and when a basket-maker completes it and turns up the ribs and starts up the sides, he must switch from working toward the left to working toward the right. "We can both do the whole basket, of course, but this way is quicker."

The basket-making tradition comes from his side of the family, as far back as any of the relatives he remembers could tell. "My mother's family, they all was white oak basket makers. My mother, she'd fill up the wagon with her baskets and go off atradin' and come back with eggs and meat and apples. Sometimes people would pay her but mostly it was tradin'. She and her mother and great-uncle and all the family way back made them for the farmers around these parts. They would put in their taters and apples and eggs and their fish when they went fishin' 'cause in those days they had nothin' else to put anything in. Lucy and me, we're the first ones to make baskets for tourists."

The Cooks lived in Colonial Williamsburg for five years, demonstrating basket-making for visitors. Mrs. Cook shows a photo taken on the scene. She wears a colonial dress and ruffled mobcap; her husband is dressed in blue knee breeches and has buckles on his shoes. Mrs. Cook liked Williamsburg, but the work was hard and Mr. Cook's health poor. "Some days eight thousand people would come through the shop!" she says. "Dad and me, we'd take us three and a half hours to make one of these half-bushel baskets, what with answering all the questions and atalkin' to folks all the while." Now a young man who was their most able apprentice has taken over the basket shop demonstrations, and the Cooks are back home.

William Cook was a farmer when Lucy married him. "He was aworkin' for one dollar a day. Then he commenced makin' baskets like his mother had taught him and right away started makin' nine dollars a week. We been amakin' them ever since, and we raised three children on basket-makin'."

"I had an uncle raised sixteen children basket-makin'. Of course things was cheap then," her husband adds. "When I started makin' baskets we had no car and we used to go out into the woods with an axe and cut down the white oak trees and carry them home on our backs, me and Lucy. All you need is a white oak tree and a axe and a wooden maul and some wooden wedges and a whittlin' knife to make baskets. This is all we ever used in our whole life. We don't use no other tools and no glue or nails or anythin'. Some does, but we just used the wood and the knife. When they're finished we don't put nothin' on them. They preserve theirselves. That's the nature of the wood."

In the back of the shed there is a

large woodpile. Mr. Cook starts a basket by splitting a green four- to eight-foot-long log in half. He uses two worn wooden wedges to split the log apart. Then each half is halved. Then the quarters are split into eighths. The heart of the wood—the darker inner part—is removed and later used for hoops and handles and sometimes for accent splits because of its darker reddish color. What's left is a billet. "Once you get to the billet you can come inside because all the rest you just use your knife on," says Mrs. Cook.

The billets are brought inside and the bark is removed with a knife. "See how I'm ahewin' on it?" Then the billet is split in half and next into fine strips. "Some says every place you split the billet it's a year's growth. Watch how I do it. I'm arunnin' the grain now, and later I go *between* the grain and you'll see the fineness you can get. When you get the split it's rough, so you got to shave it with your knife. You can get it slick as a ribbon if you want to. If you use it too rough it just makes an ugly mess."

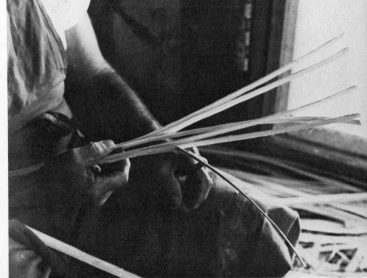

The finished splits are hung to dry and are very slightly moistened when the weaving begins. "If you really wet it, it commences to expand and when it dries it loosens again and you have an awful loose old basket."

Mr. Cook starts his half-bushel basket by cutting oak ribs, which he arranges on the table like the spokes of a wheel. The center part of each rib is narrowed down with the whittling knife. The ribs are about one and one-half inches wide and the splits generally four to six feet long. For a half-bushel-size basket the ribs are thirty-two inches long. As he begins to weave he splits each rib in half and the last one into three sections, to create an uneven number. In a few places he works in a split made of the darker heart wood. "It makes a purty pattern." Mrs. Cook works the sides.

The finished basket will be ten and one-half inches in diameter across the bottom, sixteen inches across the top, and ten inches high. The round baskets come in gallon, peck, half-bushel, and bushel sizes. Other traditional shapes include rectangular "market" baskets and larger "wash" baskets. The half-bushel size being made in these photos sells for eight dollars at the Cooks' house and for ten dollars in Williamsburg. "My mother used to get twenty-five cents for one of these if she was lucky."

The Cooks also weave chair and stool seats from white oak splits. "They'll last you about sixty years anyhow."

Are there any other white oak basket makers left in these parts?

"My brother makes a few, but he's seventy-five years old. My oldest son might be adoin' it some day. He knows how but he works as a cook now in a restaurant over by Luray Caverns. There's not much money in basket-makin'. I don't know if after me and Lucy and my brother is gone there will be anyone doin' it around here any more—makin' baskets out of the trees in the woods."

In the highlands of eastern Kentucky the traditional basket is the willow or honeysuckle "Kentucky egg basket." Originally designed to hold an even

dozen eggs, they are now made in every imaginable size. Early crafts-people flattened one side of the basket so that it could rest easily against the side of a mule. Today's baskets are rounded on the sides but retain their distinctive broad flattened bases, which permit them to stand firmly when set down on the ground.

Although they are woven in the same manner and made in the same basic shape as honeysuckle baskets, willow baskets are coarse and rough because they are made with stiff willow branches which have sharp ends. Fine, pliable honeysuckle makes a basket which is closely woven, extremely durable, and smooth enough to hold sewing fabric or knitting wool as well as produce.

Elizabeth Mills, of Stoney Fork, Kentucky, spends the long fall and winter months making fine honeysuckle baskets, which she sells to the Red Bird Mission Craft Shop, located over the next mountain in a desolate mining area. She lives with her husband, a former logger, and her eighty-five-year-old father, the chair-maker Solomon Saylor, at the far end of a remote hollow. The almost impassable road up the hollow is composed of clay and large rocks, and it crosses and recrosses the trash-filled stream on rickety plank bridges.

William Mills has not been employed since he lost his leg in a logging accident eight years ago. He often helps his wife with the basket-weaving.

Mrs. Mills explains that the honeysuckle must first be cut and scalded so that the thin bark can be removed easily by rubbing the vine with a rag. When it's time for weaving, the vines are soaked to make them pliable. Mr. Mills agrees to start a basket for his wife, and he takes two slender pieces of hickory, soaks them briefly, bends them into hoops, and fastens them with twisted wire to form the handle, rim, and base of the basket.

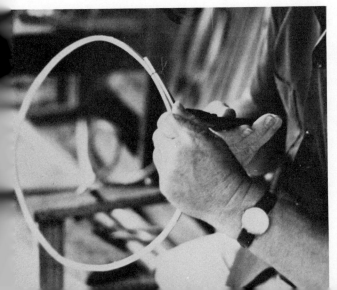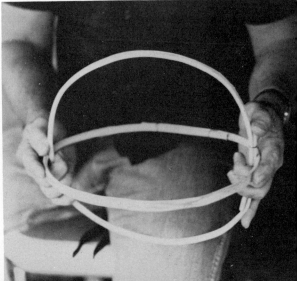

His wife takes over and weaves the corners of the basket with long pieces of the soft inner bark of the hickory tree. The bark strips look and feel like rawhide.

Next she makes ten ribs from dogwood twigs, which she whittles to a point at either end and bends to the correct curve, inserting the points under the bark corners.

When the skeleton is completed the weaving begins. Starting at one end, she weaves honeysuckle in and out through the ribs, fastening the beginning and end of each long vine by neatly weaving it in as you do in knitting. This basket, which Elizabeth Mills takes most of a day to make, will sell for about six dollars at Red Bird.

"It makes you a nice basket," she says, "but it takes a long time to make because it's wove so close. It should last you a good many years."

108

In the early 1700s when the first adventurous farmers trickled into the Appalachian highlands, basket-makers started gathering and weaving, and potters set up their kick wheels and constructed primitive kilns. The best pottery clays in the South were found in these hills, and soon the best potters discovered this fact. Their customers were their fellow pioneers, who used clay plates, crocks, jugs, and pitchers for every imaginable purpose in the house and on the farm. In these remote areas baskets, pottery, and homemade barrels were still necessities long after glass containers and metal pails and buckets became commonplace elsewhere. When Northern potters learned new manufacturing methods, their brothers in the southern mountains, isolated from other centers and craftsmen, retained their traditional techniques.

Many of the early potters had kilns similar to those used in the Far East before the Christian era. They were simply holes dug into the hillside and lined with bricks made of local clay. Some of these "groundhog" kilns, stoked with wood from the nearby forests, were still being used until recent decades. The clay was prepared in a "pug mill" turned by mule power. The mule walked round and round in a circle, harnessed to a long shaft which in turn was attached to the simple grinding boards which stirred the clay. Glazes were made of ashes, "settlin's" (silt from the creek bottom), flint, sand, ground glass when available.

Potteries tended to be family businesses. A number of old family potteries in Appalachia still exist and have maintained reputations for excellence since their founding. The Meader Pottery in northern Georgia is one famous example; the Bybee Pottery in Kentucky is another. Both have been producing traditional pots, jugs, crocks, and bowls for generations.

Just south of Asheville, North Carolina, in an area with a strong pottery tradition, Lewis Brown and his two sons, Charles and Robert, run Brown Pottery. Charles and Robert are ninth-generation potters. Their grandfather, who died within recent years, claimed that his English ancestors six generations back had been potters as well. The equipment in the pottery is all old—the huge dry pan, sifter, and pug mill, and the mammoth gas kiln, twelve feet in diameter and almost six feet high in the center. It takes thirty-six to forty-eight hours to fire pottery in this kiln to cone 3 (2,138 degrees).

All Brown's products are made of local clay with no other clays, chemicals, or minerals added. Today their best-selling wares are covered "French" pots and casseroles, glazed on the inside and unglazed on the exterior,

which their grandfather started making in the 1920s. Grandfather Brown also made ordinary flowerpots on the wheel, but the cheapness and prevalence of the factory-made variety brought an end to their production at Brown's. Grandpa also made huge pickling crocks, churns, and eight-gallon wine jugs.

Today, Charles and Robert still turn old-style bean pots, plates, jugs, and pitchers on the wheel and glaze them with the same old-fashioned brown glaze. The glaze is kept in eight-gallon handmade crocks and the pottery is dipped before firing. "Only 'ceramicists' brush on glazes," Charles says laughingly. They also make traditional face jugs, a whimsical specialty of Southern potters now bought by collectors as well as by country folk. The jug is turned on the wheel and the face modeled by hand, each

one amusingly different from the others. On a one-hundred-year-old wheel, Charles turns a jug; Robert a bowl; their father, Lewis, a bean pot. "We were always taught to stand at the wheel," Robert says.

"The important thing about our pottery," says Charles, "is that for seven generations our family has been in this country and we've all been potters. It's not just that we've known how—we've all done it for a living."

VIII ∽ SPINNING, DYEING, WEAVING, QUILTING, AND RUG-MAKING

Like other crafts in Appalachia, those involving the production and use of cloth have their roots in the pioneer past. Until one hundred years ago the intimately related crafts of spinning, vegetable dyeing, and weaving were necessary domestic skills, familiar to virtually every mountain woman. Commercial production of cloth had begun in this country in 1785, so that hand weaving was no longer the only method of making textiles, but not until late in the nineteenth century did the poor and isolated highlanders begin to make extensive use of mass-produced fabrics, abandoning their wheels and looms.

For a great many years thereafter these textile techniques were little used, until they were rediscovered and revitalized in recent decades by the crafts revival movement. But spinning, dyeing, and weaving never became entirely extinct as commonplace household activities in Appalachia. This fact is verified by the many mountain people who remember having watched their mothers and grandmothers work at the process of cloth production: planting and picking cotton and flax, tending and shearing the sheep, carding the wool, spinning, preparing dyes, weaving cloth, rugs, and coverlets.

For the pioneer woman all this was part of the daily routine. After the shearing, women and children tediously picked all burrs, bark, twigs, and other foreign matter from the wool, which was then washed and dried with great care. Cotton was picked and seeded by hand. There were no cotton gins in the mountains, and all work was done by the most primitive methods.

Spinning was accomplished at either the large "high wheel" or the small "low wheel." Cotton and wool were spun on the high wheel, which was operated by hand and required the spinner to walk back and forth. Flax and fine wool were spun on the low wheel, operated by foot pedals with the spinner seated.

Once the spinning was completed, women and children set to work digging up roots, cutting bark, picking flowers and nuts and fruit, and then preparing them for the huge, often foul-smelling iron dye pot. After the dyeing was completed the wool or thread was ready for weaving.

All the fabric was woven at home—for clothing and for bedcovers and for rugs. Linsey-woolsey was used for shirts and warm nightgowns. It was made by stringing the loom with linen warp threads and then weaving with a woolen weft—the threads carried on the shuttle which cross the warp to make the web. Cotton twill, used for work jeans, was usually dyed gray or blue. Other cottons, often woven in simple checked or striped patterns, were made into every type of clothing for adults and children.

A survey in 1810 found that there were 17,316 hand looms still in use in Tennessee, despite the fact that by this date the mechanized textile industry was well under way. Mrs. A. Barnes displayed what was probably a not uncommon range of abilities when she took prizes at an 1855 state fair for her weaving of fine jeans, brown jeans, cotton coverlets, flannel, striped cotton, flax, linen, tow linen, and linen diaper.

There was another alternative to manufactured fabrics, and that was the work of professional weavers. When Mrs. Barnes ran off with all the prizes at the fair, there were twenty-five professional weavers in Tennessee, the majority immigrants from Great Britain and Switzerland. Transportation was so poor and the economy so depressed that home weaving as a financial necessity continued in many parts of the state well into the twentieth century.

Mrs. Golda Porter, a hale and cheerful widow who lives in Virginia at the foot of Banner Mountain, is an expert spinner, dyer, and weaver. She spins wool, flax, rabbit hair, goat hair, and even dog hair on her small flax wheel, which was made in 1870 and has been in continuous use ever since. She says that many pet lovers save the clippings when they trim their dogs and send them to her by the bagful for spinning. One customer knit herself a sweater with wool Mrs. Porter spun from the clippings from her dog. As a knitter Mrs. Porter finds homespun much pleasanter to work with than commercial yarn. "It's just nicer somehow. It's not stretchy, and the unevenness, the little bumps you get hand spinning, make the feel and look more interesting, don't you think?"

The carding process, a necessary step in spinning, stretches and straightens the fiber. The cards themselves are wooden paddles covered with fine wire prongs. After carding, Mrs. Porter has a long fluffy rope of wool, which she then begins to feed through the hollow spindle of her wheel.

The action of the wheel twists and tightens the fibers, transforming them into thread or yarn. On the flax wheel the thickness of the yarn is limited by the size of the opening in the spindle.

The oldest woven fabrics from these mountains were made of wool dyed with indigo (blue) and madder (red). Both these dye plants were used in either their wild or their cultivated form. Madder gave a range of colors from a bright or dark red to a soft delicate pink and was often combined with other plants for color variation. Lavenders came from pokeberries; grays and beiges from sumac berries; green from pine needles; blacks and grays from walnut bark, butternut hulls, witch hazel, or sourwood bark. The bark of the sycamore gave a slate gray, beech bark combined with witch hazel a particular blue, sassafras root and bark a red-brown, and sassafras flowers a bright yellow. Rhododendron leaves turned the dye pot purplish gray, bay leaf or peach leaf a bright yellow.

An old recipe for "setting a blue pot" instructed housewives to put two ounces of indigo into a little sack and soak it for twelve hours. A half-bushel pot of water was to be warmed on the fire and the indigo then rubbed through the sack into the warm water. The other ingredients to be added were a little madder, a teacup of wheat bran, and a half pint of lye. The pot was to be kept warm but not boiling until the dye turned green and foamy, a process which took several days. For a pale blue color the wool was to be dipped about five times, for a deeper color many more. It was then necessary to wash the wool in clear warm water to remove the lye, which would otherwise rot the wool. Other vegetable dyes were much simpler to prepare, but the indigo blue remained a favorite.

Anyone interested in natural dyes must be something of a botanist. Golda Porter goes "agatherin'" whenever the time is right." She knows each flower and nut and berry that grows, and she picks each in season. "The woods here have everything," she says. "You can get real purty colors, so much more meller than chemical dyes." She bubbles up pots of yellows, oranges, and browns from goldenrod flowers, onion skins, walnut hulls. For red she gathers madder and pokeberries, for blue there is indigo. For green, she says, just mix indigo and goldenrod, of course! Onion skin and indigo make another shade of green. Elderberry and maple bark will both give you a fine purple. She gathers lichens from the rocks and is amazed at the variety of unexpected colors they can produce.

Recently she dyed some yellow wool with goldenrod that had just come into bloom. She stripped the flowers from the stems, boiled them until an ooze formed, skimmed off the ooze, and added table salt to set the color. She proudly exhibits a lap full of homespun yellow wool. She uses the recipes of her ancestors, despite the fact that she finds it considerably easier to cook up her potions on her electric stove than she would in an iron pot over a wood fire.

After the dyeing comes the weaving, always the most enjoyable part of textile production. Mrs. Porter weaves traditional fabrics, coverlets, and rugs—a rug is in process right now. She also enjoys making more contemporary items—napkins and place mats and novelties such as corn husk mats, in which colored cotton thread is the warp and strips of dried corn husk the weft.

Warm woolen coverlets—made on the loom—and patchwork quilts—made with a needle—were the two types of bedclothing used in the mountains, and both were made with considerable care and pride. They were often the most colorful objects in the austere mountain cabins and were intended to be used for years and handed down to the next generation. Woven coverlets have always been considered the great *tour de force* of the home weaver's skill. They have been treasured heirlooms and have become collectors' prizes because of their attractiveness and the difficulty of the work. The coverlet patterns had remarkable names: Wide World's Wonder, Sunrise on the Walls of Troy, Star of Venus, Wonder of the Forest, Captured Beauty, Star of the East, Flourishing Wave, Sally's Fancy, Pansies and Roses in the Wilderness, Queen's Delight, Islands of the Sea, Rose in the Garden, and many more. One interesting coverlet pattern is strangely named Bonaparte's Retreat.

When starting a coverlet the weaver must first wind the cotton thread on spools, carefully measuring. It must then be put on the beam of the loom with each thread led through the eyes of the "heedles" which hang vertically from the horizontal "harness." Weaving jeans or linsey-woolsey requires two harnesses; coverlets require four to eight, and seven to eight hundred warp threads. The harness is raised and lowered by the foot treadles. Depending on which treadle is pressed by the weaver's foot, one or another set of warp threads is raised, making the pattern as the shuttle crosses through the web.

The coverlet patterns were written on "drafts"—narrow pieces of paper which varied between four and twenty inches in length, depending on the pattern. The draft, inscribed on the paper in a type of notation meaningless to anyone but a weaver, recorded one unit of the pattern. Sometimes slashed lines in various combinations were used on the drafts; often one finds a combination of lines and figures. The draft was fastened on the front of the loom and when not in use was carefully rolled and tied. Collections of old drafts are kept in museums today, and they bear frequent pinpricks where the weaver kept her place if called suddenly from her work to mind her kettle or her child.

Three types of coverlets were made in the mountains in pioneer times, and the techniques are preserved today by a few elderly people and in crafts revival centers. The first and most common was the "overshot" weave, the term for cotton warp "overshot" with woolen weft. The "summer and winter weave" shows a reversed design. If the pattern is brown on a white ground, the other side will come out with the pattern white on a brown ground. The "double weave" is also reversed in this fashion, but it consists of two interwoven webs which can be separated by the fingers.

All the old coverlets were made on looms which permitted a maximum width of about forty-four inches, and the pattern was carefully designed to come together in the center, where the two widths necessary for a bed-cover were seamed. Only in commercial production was it possible to achieve a coverlet eighty-five or ninety inches wide which was all one piece. It is a simple matter to distinguish old homemade bedcovers from the manufactured item by looking for this seam.

Taft Greer, a distinguished weaver, lives at the peak of a tall mountain in Trade, Tennessee. The farmers sitting around chatting in the country store recommend that the best way to find his house is by helicopter. The road up the mountain is alarmingly steep but passable. Mr. Greer lives there because he was born there and his ancestors likewise.

"Those old settlers liked mountaintops," he says. "They were easier to clear because the trees were smaller." His modest house is located close to another house—a log structure which is now in a state of total collapse. "I was born in that house," he says, pointing to the ruined old cabin. "I learned about dyeing and weaving from my grandmother when I was a boy."

Nancy Osborne Greer was a skilled craftswoman who was still spinning cotton and wool for her loom at the age of one hundred. She died in 1934, in the old log cabin she had come to as a bride eighty years earlier. She did her spinning throughout her married life on a wheel which had been a wedding gift from her mother-in-law. Her loom, which Taft Greer uses today, is a heavy-timbered homemade instrument which Nancy Greer inherited from *her* grandmother. Her grandson estimates its date of construction as 1801.

Today the loom, which used to be kept in the log house, virtually fills a work shed near the Greers' tobacco field. On it Taft Greer still weaves a few exquisite coverlets in the Wall of Jericho pattern, which was his grandmother's favorite. The loom is fully strung, and he begins a coverlet, using white wool and a soft brown wool which he dyed with elderberries. "You can get three or four colors of brown out of walnut hulls, elderberry, and bloodroot," he says. Hanging from the ceiling of the shed is some white wool he hasn't dyed yet.

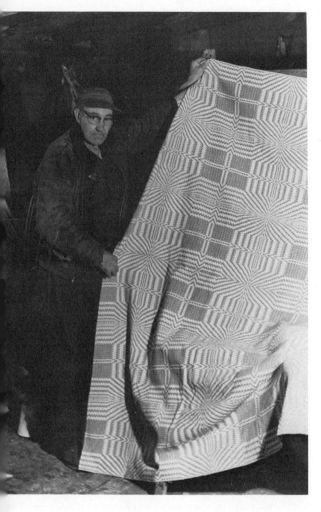

Greer still finds weaving a satisfying occupation, but he no longer depends on it as his main source of income. Tobacco growing is more profitable, and when spring comes he abandons his loom. "I have seven children and none of them want to weave," he says. "This coverlet sells for fifty dollars and takes me six days at least. Young people want to earn more money." He agrees graciously, but with some shyness, to hold up a finished coverlet for the camera. "I'll maybe do some more weaving come winter, God willing."

Outside the shed Mrs. Greer is chopping firewood. Her hatchet makes the only sound in this remote spot. "It's a good place to live," he says. He motions with embarrassment to several abandoned automobiles near the house. "I have to clean it up, get these taken off. When I was a boy the road up this mountain was so bad that I couldn't go to school and that's a hard thing." He indicates the dirt road of 1973. "It was a bad road. I learned to write purty good anyhow when I was a boy, but you know how it is. If you don't do something all the time you just forget it. I suppose if I'd worked in an office—kept it up, you know—but when you just live your life up on the mountain farmin' and weavin' you don't have no use for writin' and you forget how to do it. You see how it is? . . . Come back. Come back and set and talk awhile. I'm going to clean up . . . get rid of these old cars that looks so awful."

Although the Appalachian coverlet is relatively unfamiliar to outsiders, virtually everyone knows and appreciates patchwork quilts. Surely it would astound and amuse the countrywomen of a hundred years ago to know that quilts are now being displayed with great fanfare in museums; that they are prominent favorites in exhibits of Americana; that they are being avidly sought by collectors and connoisseurs who are willing to pay the highest prices.

After all, making bed coverings was always the most thrifty and commonplace of all the traditional crafts. A quilt is simply an envelope made of two pieces of cloth, which is filled with fluffy batting and then stitched through all three layers with a running stitch so that they stay together. Quilts were made by all pioneer women to serve a basic need. The fact that intricate decorative quilting patterns developed, that the work also served as a release for creative expression, and that the finished product was frequently delightful to behold—all this was incidental.

Because they were traditionally made of scraps, often cut from garments which had already had considerable wear, few quilts remain from the Revolutionary or pre-Revolutionary period, and many of the finest Victorian examples are simply fragile lengths of esteemed tatters, still tenuously held together. But although factory-made bedcovers became widely available around 1890, the art of quilting never died out, and a great many American families of vastly different social and economic backgrounds have in their possession quilts made by a still living or vividly remembered grandmother or great-grandmother.

Anyone who enjoys stitchery at all can appreciate the aesthetic gratification women through the ages have felt in piecing together bits and pieces of colorful cotton fabric to make the exuberant patterns which became traditional. Additionally, quilting served a social function. Quilting bees were enormously convivial occasions in Appalachia as well as in other rural areas of the country. The hostess would "put in" a quilt on her frame and invite a group of women—no more than could fit on chairs placed around the sides of the frame. They would chat and sew and exchange opinions, patterns, and scraps, working together on a quilt that might be destined to be a gift for a new bride, a poor elderly neighbor, a newborn child. By evening the quilt would be complete and the men would arrive for dinner or a square dance.

The pleasure of making and owning quilts was so widespread that even in families where there was no economic necessity for using up old rags to make something warm for the bed, women pieced their own bright covers. Some of the most elaborate and elegant quilts were sewn by the wives of wealthy Southern plantation owners. For the daughters of the rich, private lessons in embroidery and fine quilting were advertised in newspapers. For almost everyone, there was readily available instruction from a mother, grandmother, or aunt who had learned the old patterns from *her* female forebears. The simplest and rudest cabins were invariably graced and livened by their creations and by handsome braided, hooked, or woven rugs, also made from outworn or outgrown clothing.

At first all of the fabric used was homespun, home-dyed, and hand-woven material, but later brightly colored cotton calico fabrics were widely manufactured. In cutting out clothes from these bolts of cotton every scrap was saved for the quilting basket. If a rural housewife had bits and pieces of wool and perhaps even a scrap of silk or velvet as well, she didn't attempt one of the usual patterns but instead made herself a "crazy quilt" composed of a mixture of odd-shaped scraps sewed together and then featherstitched or briarstitched on top. These humblest of quilts are now particular favorites of many collectors.

The old patterns have exuberant suggestive names taken from rural life or biblical lore. They are more descriptive and less romantic than the names of woven coverlet patterns: Jacob's Ladder, Log Cabin, Hearts and Gizzards, Feathered Star, Chips and Whetstones, Rose of Sharon, Crown of Thorns, Delectable Mountain, Bear's Paw, Robbing Peter to Pay Paul, Barn Raising, Straight Furrow, Dove-in-the-Window, Wild Goose Chase, Drunkard's Path.

Patchwork can be fashioned in two very different ways: pieced or appliquéd. Pieced quilts have been much the more common at all times. Some quilts, however, are partly pieced and partly appliquéd and, less commonly, a quilt may be further enhanced by cross-stitch embroidery.

This traditional pieced top is being made by Mrs. Ora Watson of Banner Elk, North Carolina, wife of the toy-maker Willard Watson. "I don't never do appliqué," Mrs. Watson says, "just pieced quilts." The quilt she's working on is a pattern called Star of Bethlehem, and it's one of her favorites.

First she cuts her scraps and stitches them together to form one square of her pattern. "Here's the right side and here's the wrong side where the seams is. The next thing you do is just sit comfortable and sew it all together to make the top. When that's done I take my backing and put it on the frame, take my padding and put that on top of the backing, then put my pieced top on. Then I just start quiltin'."

She shows the quilt on her frame in another room. "First it just about fills the whole room, but you work quiltin' in from the sides and you keep rollin' it so's you can get to the center. This one, hit's about half finished."

With understandable pride she holds up a recently completed Star of Bethlehem quilt. "You want to make a quilt?" she asks. "You got a needle and thread? That's all you need."

Mrs. Watson uses a traditionally simple frame. Four strips of wood are fastened in a square with clamped corners, and the frame can be either suspended from ceiling wires or rested on chairs. Heavy cloth is tacked to the edges of the frame and the three layers of the quilt are basted or pinned to this fabric. As the quilting progresses the clamps are released and the edges of the quilt wound around them.

Emma Glotfelty lives with her energetic eighty-four-year-old husband in a trim new house surrounded by fields of corn near the town of Accident, Maryland. She is a precise and patient Mennonite lady who makes handsome quilts. The one on her frame right now is a pattern called Double Irish Chain. Like many contemporary quilters she uses Dacron filling and is careful that all scraps are colorfast for easy washing and drying. For her backing she uses a white sheet.

"My mother made quilts like this for all of us—we were eight children," she says wistfully. "She cut up our old clothes for the scraps and when we looked at our bed coverings we remembered that particular dress or shirt or nightgown. Now I'm making them for my children and grandchildren."

She shows a quilt her mother made several decades ago and points to a repeated square in a soft blue fabric with white flowers. "I remember this dress. It was one of Mother's and I liked it particularly."

Mrs. Glotfelty has been successful in competitions. "They look at the way you miter the corners and miter the binding in the corners. They're interested in the fineness of the stitches, choice of colors, width of the border. My—they're exacting!"

Martha Housewright is an elderly countrywoman who lives on the steep side of a mountain outside Church Hill, Tennessee. Her rough quilting frame fills the entire sitting room of her small house. On the frame is a quilt of traditional Wedding Ring pattern. Mrs. Housewright appliqués, rather than piecing, the top.

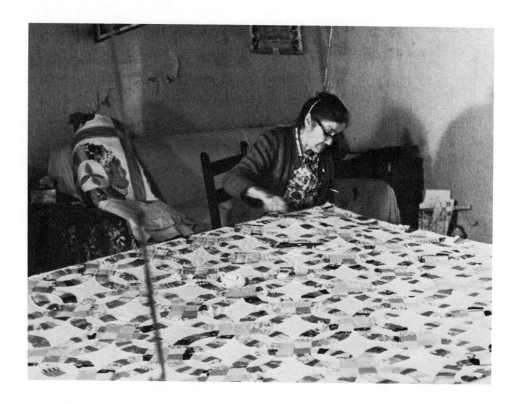

"You do it easy enough. You take a square of white domestic and then you cut your scraps in the right shape and then just hemstitch 'em onto the white. We call the stuffin' 'mountain mist cloth.' I don't know what others call it. When I get my top appliquéd I put my backing on the frame and my mountain mist stuffin' and my top and I set here and quilt."

128

She carries another quilt out to the porch. "This here's almost finished. I took hit off the frame last week and I just have to put on the binding. This pattern you call Wagon Wheel. Everybody's got his own taste but I like this best."

Rug-making, like quilting, is an honored pioneer craft which has never required the impetus of a revival to keep it viable. When factory-produced carpets became available the thrifty housewives of Appalachia continued to braid, hook, and weave. Using materials which would otherwise be discarded—burlap sacks emptied of their sugar or grain, and rag strips cut from used clothing—the isolated farm women made brightly colored durable rugs to warm and grace the rough wooden floors of their simple cabins. Today most of the braiding, hooking, and weaving of rugs in the southern highlands is being done by older women who remember watching their mothers, grandmothers, and aunts busy themselves with the same soothing, repetitive motions of rug-making.

Rugs are popular items in Appalachian crafts shops, because their sturdy honest attractiveness appeals to people of widely varied tastes. They blend well with country antiques or contemporary decor, enhance a living room as well as a bedroom, and when made well may be expected to last, as mountain women say, "from now on."

Three entirely different methods of rug-making have been commonly practiced here and in other rural areas. All three depend on a good supply of castoff clothing—and little else. Braided rugs, most commonly oval in shape, require only rags, a needle, and some strong thread. Hooked rugs are made by attaching a rectangular piece of burlap to a simple wooden frame and then pulling loops of material up from the underside to the upper side with a hook attached to a wooden handle. Woven rugs, made on looms, use the same sort of rag strips wound around a shuttle as the weft material, and strong cotton cords as the warp. Both the woven and braided rugs have the added attraction of being completely reversible, while the hooked rugs offer more of a challenge to artistic rug-makers who want to copy or design a picture or pattern.

Anna Weir is a prolific rug-hooker. She is a hearty good-natured woman who drives the mail truck along the rural routes outside the town of Lanaconing, Maryland, near the West Virginia border—a job she has held for the past eighteen years. Lanaconing used to be a busy mining center, but now most of the activity is in mechanized strip mining and the young men are more likely to seek employment in the four industrial plants nearby.

"It's an Indian name, Lanaconing. It means a place where five waters meet," says Mrs. Weir.

"And there *is* five waters ameetin' here," adds her sister, Clara Pierce. Both women are coal miners' widows.

"The town used to be altogether different," Mrs. Weir says. "Now there's no movie theater, no entertainment 'cept the Senior Citizens' Square Dance."

"The young folks go there too," says Mrs. Pierce, "'cause there isn't any other place to go. The boys get married—like mine—at eighteen, because there's no place to take a date!"

"In the old days when pay night came for the miners, 'Coning—that's what we call Lanaconing—was lit up like a Christmas tree! There was just *lots* of things going on. Of course now the old miners is mostly all dead of the black lung," she adds.

Mrs. Weir's truck is parked in front of her hillside home. It's 10 A.M. and she has finished her first route and has a few hours before she starts the second, which will take the rest of her day. Mrs. Pierce, who makes braided rugs, has brought one along to work on. "My youngest boy, he used to hook rugs," she says. "He hooked more than my girls. He was always doin' things and when it was good he was out huntin' and when it was cold he was in hookin'. Our mother did hooked rugs and plaited rugs and tattin' and crochetin'. She always said tattin' was the hardest."

Mrs. Weir has a partially worked rug on her hooking frame. "I saw the pattern in a vision," she explains. "I see lots of visions. You get them just when you wake up. I see beautiful buildings and shining garments like we don't know about down here on the earth. I seen Jesus several times. This pattern was a vision and I kept it in my mind for a long time and then I decided I would make it. So I put it up on the frame on Monday and drawed it up and since then I kept my nose to it purty good. I'm making the background all gray because I have this big old coat to cut up."

Rug-hooking can be done with yarn or with rags, but Mrs. Weir, like most mountain women, works exclusively with rags. She saves old clothes, and her friends and relatives save theirs. She also goes to rummage sales and buys worn-out garments. "I used to take old sheets and tear them up and dye them, but now I don't use cotton, just woolen rags made from old clothes."

The small living room is filled with rugs and mats of various vintages. "This one our mother did—this is Clara's daughter's rug—my son made this one—I made this last winter when we had all the snow."

Mrs. Weir flips a few of them over to show their backing. "It's burlap. I use old sacks. My son has some cows and I take his cattle feed sacks. That's what Mother always did. I'd say to her, 'Let's put a rug in,' and we'd go out to the barn and cut up a big sack. This here rug I put up on what used to be my mother-in-law's frame. I just got me a sack and I decided to do that design I seen in my vision."

She takes one of the long narrow strips of woolen cloth and holds it below the burlap with her left hand. With her right hand she pokes her hook in and lifts a small loop of fabric up above the burlap. The hook pokes in again and comes up with another loop, just below the first. Rows of hooking follow rapidly and evenly.

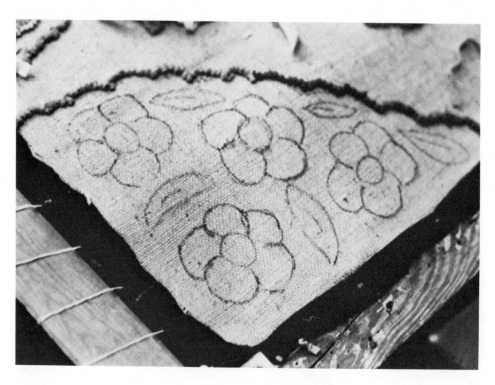

"Some folks goes up and down, some diagonal. It doesn't matter. I just do my design first and then fill in the background. You got to sew the binding on first because that's how you get it fixed to the frame. Then you just keep ahookin' till you're finished."

She looks at the rug with satisfaction. "This rug will hold up pretty substantial," she says.

Mrs. Pierce sits by the window making a seven-piece "plait" for her braided rug. She, too, haunts the rummage sales and keeps bags filled with scraps of cloth.

"Hooked rugs lays better," she explains. "With a braided rug sometimes it humps up in the middle. You have to be careful when you sew it together so that doesn't happen. The way you do, you start with a two-piece plait for the center—real narrow. You coil it around real careful so's it's flat. Then you work up to three plaits, and gradual-like up to seven. Then you have to decrease at the end back to two plaits so it has an even edge. That's the trick. The seven-plait makes a nice thick piece so there's less sewin'. I used to make three-plaits, but my eyes is terrible. I'm legally blind, you know. Sometimes I make them as big as thirteen plaits so's to have less sewin'." She demonstrates the mysterious skill of making a braid with thirteen strands.

"You don't have to see to plait when you been doin' it all your life, but this here sewin' needle—that's proper little!"

Fine woven rugs seem to be something of a specialty with the craftswomen of western Maryland. Among the best are those made by Emma Glotfelty, the quilt-maker.

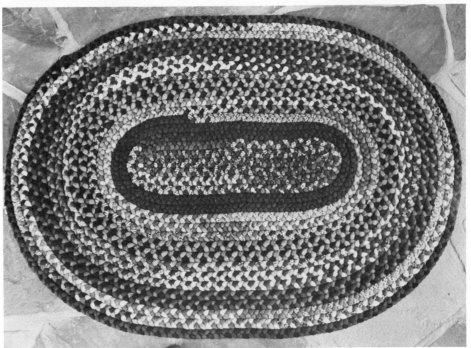

Mrs. Glotfelty makes rugs out of cotton and wool, but she never combines different fabrics. "I've made them out of rayon, too—old rayon curtains—and they're right nice, but you must do all cotton or all rayon or all wool." She is rightfully proud of her work and shows a large stack of rugs. Her loom will turn out a rug a yard wide, but she rarely exceeds twenty-seven inches. "I can make them right long," she says, "but most are about a yard and a half. That's a good size."

The loom is threaded with a special carpet warp in two colors, red and green. "You can make the warp—we call it the 'chain'—in any color you like. Often I alternate three or four colors so that when you look at the rug at the end you can see first a red thread, then a yellow, then a blue, then a green." She shows a carpet where this has been done.

The rags are cut on the bias and the rough edges are turned under when the rag is tightly wound in a ball. "That's one secret of how to make a really nice-looking rug. The other is to weave it good and tight. Why, I've seen some rugs wove so loose you could put a finger through it. I really hit each row with the reed good and hard so it's right up tight against the last row. That makes them really firm."

She sits at the loom and runs the shuttle back and forth between the colored cords. The shuttle is wound with long strips, about a quarter inch wide, of a pleasing pale blue fabric. She pulls the batten forward at the end of each row with great vigor, pressing the reed against the new row as hard as she can. To finish the ends she weaves carpet thread back and forth through a half-inch length of warp threads and then makes tassels of added lengths of the brightly colored cord. Some of her rugs have stripes of every imaginable hue; others are austere contemporary-looking two-colored jobs. A small white and brown rug is particularly handsome.

"My mother and aunts made woven rugs," she reminisces. "They had huge old looms and they did carpets that could just about fill a room. They only let me make the rags. They would never let me weave. I would take the old cotton work pants and cut the rags and wind the strips into balls. They would wind them onto the shuttle and turn them into rugs while I watched and watched and wanted to weave. You know, I never did do it either until after my mother died and I was lonely and I decided to take up some rug weaving. I'd been quilting, but never weaving when I was young."

TODAY AND TOMORROW

In houses, cabins, sheds, and workshops along new four-lane roads and on washed-out paths through remote hills and hollows, the men and women of the southern highlands are practicing crafts for pleasure and for profit. In attractive crafts shops and at a host of fairs a scattering of old-time basketmakers and weavers exhibit their wares alongside those of young college-trained silk screen artists, sculptors, ceramicists, stained glass workers. Many people, old and young, are receiving assistance and instruction through a number of privately and publicly funded agencies. In one project handicapped Appalachian artisans are making up-dated "country furniture" under the direction of top-flight designers. The Southern Highlands Handicrafts Guild, started in 1930, runs classes, shops, exhibits, and fairs in several states. At colleges and cooperatives—including Berea College in Kentucky, where the first efforts toward a crafts revival began at the end of the last century—the most skilled professional training is offered to people interested in new and old-style handicrafts.

In the state of West Virginia the crafts are particularly highly organized. The West Virginia Artists and Craftsmen's Guild has four hundred members who have joined together to promote and market their products. An arts and crafts division in the state's chamber of commerce sponsors fairs and offers educational and technical assistance. Along with O.E.O. it has sponsored such projects as Mountain Artisans of Charleston, which now lists several hundred West Virginia women who work in local cooperatives making patchwork quilts and fashions to be sold in shops around the country.

New ideas utilizing old techniques have resulted in such easily saleable products as patchwork pillows and stuffed animals. These pillows were made by members of a nonprofit cooperative named Cabin Creek Quilts, organized by VISTA in 1970 to assist elderly and low-income women of West Virginia. The patchwork animals are sold by the Rural Arts and Crafts Association, which markets the work of craftspeople from six West Virginia counties.

Although an array of handsome crafts products never previously associated with the southern mountain region are admired at the new crafts shops and fairs, many of the old favorites remain best-sellers. At the West

Virginia Mountain Heritage Arts and Crafts Festival in Harpers Ferry, Dick Schnacke's booth was a leading crowd pleaser. Schnacke employs over forty West Virginia craftsmen who work in their own homes making traditional mountain toys including the giant limberjack, the corn cob pigs, and the climbing bear. The whimmydiddle—simplest of Appalachian toys— was photographed at the Penn-Alps Crafts shop in Grantsville, Maryland. You can make it spin to the right or the left once you've learned the trick of controlling the propeller. Just call out, as you would to your mule, "Gee!" (right) or "Haw!" (left)—and off it will go. Backwoodsmen have been whittling them for their children as far back as anyone can remember, along with wooden tops, whistles, and pea shooters. The old playthings retain their charm and appeal in a crafts scene studded with glossier, more sophisticated, and more costly wares.

The crafts are changing in Appalachia to meet the realities of today's markets, so that the full economic potential of the movement may be realized for the benefit of people in the country's most depressed areas. Inevitably, there are few people left who spend all day on a five-dollar honeysuckle basket or over a week on a fifty-dollar coverlet. Part of the purpose of this book has been to record the passing of certain traditional crafts and techniques which rose not from the demands of shoppers, but from the practical needs of an earlier time. Machines, combined with a greater or lesser degree of hand labor, are being increasingly employed by craftsmen. More and more commonly, artists and designers from distant metropolitan areas are being applauded for creating new "Appalachian" products.

Much has been lost, but valid realistic goals are being attained. The therapeutic and financial rewards of making attractive high-quality products for sale is relieving the financial despair of many of the region's elders and reinforcing the new, proudly independent Appalachian nationalism of many of the young. The sturdy crafts tradition is alive and well in Appalachia.

ABOUT THE AUTHOR AND PHOTOGRAPHERS

ELINOR LANDER HORWITZ was born in New Haven, Connecticut, and was graduated from Smith College. Her marriage to neurosurgeon Norman Horwitz took her to Chevy Chase, Maryland, where they now live. The Horwitzes are avid collectors of books, Persian miniatures, and Islamic pottery, and Elinor, an amateur sculptor, achieved a claim to immortality when her gargoyle was accepted for the face of the National Cathedral in Washington, D.C.

Professionally, Elinor Lander Horwitz has written for many major national magazines and is a regular feature writer for the Washington, D.C., *Evening Star News*. She is the author of a number of books for young people.

Anthony and Joshua Horwitz are dedicated amateur photographers who accompanied their mother on her travels through Appalachia to take the pictures for this book.